# POETRY NOW
# EASTERN ENGLAND 2003

Edited by

Heather Killingray

First published in Great Britain in 2002 by
*POETRY NOW*
Remus House,
Coltsfoot Drive,
Peterborough, PE2 9JX
Telephone (01733) 898101
Fax (01733) 313524

All Rights Reserved

*Copyright Contributors 2002*

HB ISBN 0 75434 381 2
SB ISBN 0 75434 382 0

# *Foreword*

Although we are a nation of poets we are accused of not reading poetry, or buying poetry books. After many years of listening to the incessant gripes of poetry publishers, I can only assume that the books they publish, in general, are books that most people do not want to read.

Poetry should not be obscure, introverted, and as cryptic as a crossword puzzle: it is the poet's duty to reach out and embrace the world.

The world owes the poet nothing and we should not be expected to dig and delve into a rambling discourse searching for some inner meaning.

The reason we write poetry (and almost all of us do) is because we want to communicate: an ideal; an idea; or a specific feeling. Poetry is as essential in communication, as a letter; a radio; a telephone, and the main criterion for selecting the poems in this anthology is very simple: they communicate.

# CONTENTS

| | | |
|---|---|---|
| Treading On Dolphins | Fran Harris | 1 |
| Untitled | C Woolmore | 1 |
| Stambourne | Patricia E Woodley | 2 |
| The Bar Is A Garden | Keith L Powell | 2 |
| The Power Of Now | Geraldine Sanders | 3 |
| Norfolk Grave | Trish Duxbury | 4 |
| My Child | Tara Borg | 5 |
| A Lincolnshire Landscape | Una McLean-Manning | 6 |
| I Cannot Cope | Wila Yagel | 7 |
| January Morning | John Guy | 8 |
| The Harbour Mouth | Sue Cooper | 9 |
| Sail Away | Jodie Bradshaw | 10 |
| What Did You Do In The War Daddy? | Jacqueline Ellen Boorman | 11 |
| My Garden | Daisy Gilson | 12 |
| Observations From A Train Window | Edna D'Lima | 12 |
| Trying To Keep Healthy | Olive Peck | 13 |
| The Right Move | Sheila Buckingham | 14 |
| Through Kyle's Eyes | Elizabeth Farrow | 14 |
| A Winner's Game | Julia McNeill | 15 |
| Small Is Beautiful | Aves Swanson | 16 |
| In Summertime | Nigel Lloyd Maltby | 17 |
| Independent Woman | Emma Graham | 18 |
| Tupholme Abbey | David Radford | 18 |
| Powerful Forces | Lilian Owen | 19 |
| Bells For The Bridge | S P Springthorpe | 20 |
| Memories | Barbara King | 20 |
| Ode To Norfolk | Beryl D Graham | 21 |
| King's Lynn - Old And New | Kathy Jordan | 22 |
| Let's Dance | Anne Hornigold | 23 |
| Dangerous Gift | Anne Sanderson | 24 |
| The Violinist | Winifred Booth | 25 |
| A Hand To Hold | G Walklett | 26 |
| The Warm Glow | Erica Sillett | 26 |
| Passing Through | A J Spencer | 27 |

| | | |
|---|---|---|
| Why? | E Harrod | 27 |
| Regrets | C B Walklett | 28 |
| The Slipper Chapel | Olive Poole | 28 |
| At Season's Close | Lyn Sandford | 29 |
| Blackbird Ditty | Pam Dutton | 30 |
| Sound Becomes Silence | Simon Richardson | 31 |
| In My Dreams | David Duthie | 32 |
| Looking At A Dead Man's Things | Rebecca Goss | 33 |
| A Beautiful Place | Suzanne Reeves | 34 |
| A Word Of Advice? | H B Walklett | 34 |
| Delirium | D Morgan | 35 |
| Pictures In the Fire | Pat Coldwell | 36 |
| Those Were The Days | M F Base | 37 |
| Essex | John Bracken | 38 |
| Prayer For East Anglia | Carl Waite | 39 |
| Untitled | Lew Park | 40 |
| Snowflakes | Gordon Finlay | 40 |
| In My Norfolk - The Sound Of Music | E Barker | 41 |
| Robert | Jacqueline Hartnett | 41 |
| The Invisible Cord | Maureen Ayling | 42 |
| Hadleigh Castle | Arthur Allen | 43 |
| The Next Morning | Paul Kelly | 44 |
| Memories | Duchess Newman | 45 |
| Yesterday's Child | Helen T Westley | 46 |
| Night Of The Full Moon | H S Persse | 46 |
| A Question Of Poetry | Rosiane Walklett | 47 |
| Whiteout | Andrew Sanders | 48 |
| I've Lost My Dog | Judith Hill | 49 |
| Suffer Little Children | Lynda Fordham | 50 |
| Hand In Hand | Christine Lemon | 51 |
| A Very English Summer | Jon Oyster | 52 |
| Cherish Your Childhood | Graeme Vine | 53 |
| The Path Of Life | Joan Picton | 54 |
| Forever Love | Kate Long | 55 |
| Feeling | Joanna Smith | 55 |
| 1953 | Beryl Sigournay | 56 |

| Title | Author | Page |
|---|---|---|
| Life | Racheal Shanks | 56 |
| Home Counties Essex South East | E Norman | 57 |
| In The Future | S B Kershaw | 58 |
| Anticipating Summer | Barnaby Lockyer | 60 |
| Swimming In The Mud | Katherine Lunn | 61 |
| Desensitised | Lorna Walklett | 62 |
| The Story Of Life | Darren Ferguson | 64 |
| The Bungalow | Joy Lennick | 65 |
| Adoption | Pamela Matthews | 66 |
| Out Of The Blue | U Johnson | 66 |
| The Beach | John Talman | 67 |
| Why? | Trina Mayes | 67 |
| Mobile Lovesong | J Oliver | 68 |
| Flames Of Love | Janet Mills | 69 |
| Music Of The Mind | Catherine May | 70 |
| The Court Of Owls | Richard Maslen | 71 |
| Time | V M Seaman | 72 |
| If | Richard Lee Nettleton | 72 |
| Centipede In The Sky | Jean Rosemary Regan | 73 |
| Questions And Answers | Farrell & Wright | 74 |
| Chilton Brook, Hundon, Suffolk | Yvonne Elizabeth Hicks | 74 |
| Winter | Joan Hammond | 75 |
| Sovereign Of The Sky | Corinda Daw | 76 |
| The Accident | Duchess Newman | 77 |
| My Norfolk | Helen Lock | 78 |
| A Helping Hand | H Willmott | 78 |
| Donkey Friends | Mary Rose | 79 |
| Special Moments | Michelle Luetchford | 80 |
| An Eastern Promise? | John E Day | 81 |
| Dialogue | Rosemary Harvey | 82 |
| Dear Grandpa | Luke Blurton | 83 |
| Message To A PE Teacher | Pamela Morton | 84 |
| Husband, Dad And Friend | Siân Blurton | 85 |
| The Red Intruder | Sylvia Horder | 86 |
| Love Poetry | Paul Divine | 86 |
| Visitors | Margaret Adams | 87 |
| Attics Of My Heart | Robin E Edwards | 88 |
| Norfolk Retreats | John Coleridge | 89 |

| | | |
|---|---|---|
| The Country Bus Comedians | D M Harvey | 90 |
| The Golden Jubilee | Sue Vince | 91 |
| Dance The Viennese Waltz | Colin Shaw | 92 |
| Hotel Study | Laurence D E Calvert | 93 |
| Missing | Margaret Meagher | 94 |
| An Eye For An Eye | Jocelyn Benham | 95 |
| Southwold | Alison Housden | 96 |
| A Grandmother's Thoughts | Pat Haywood | 97 |
| Set Me Free | Susan Abdulrahman | 98 |
| Tempus Fugit | Sue Desney-Hudson | 98 |
| Those Were The Days, Son | S Rouse | 99 |
| Paper Chase | Kathryn West | 100 |
| Secret Shame | Annette Murphy | 101 |
| Suffolk | Samantha Pryke | 102 |
| First Light | Eddie Lawrence | 103 |
| Barbara | Barbara Goode | 104 |
| One More Time | Susan Watson | 105 |
| A Cantabrigian Abroad | J M Jones | 106 |
| Spring 1985 | Edith Tyrrell | 106 |
| My Prayer | Jenny Johnson | 107 |
| A Very Special Occasion | I L Wright | 107 |
| Crossing Fen Country | David Xeno | 108 |
| Jesus Green | Hannah Langworth | 108 |
| Celtic Man | Carmel Wright | 109 |
| An Honest Luck | Tiffany Tondut | 110 |
| Thorpe Meadows | A R Cubitt | 111 |
| Poverty At Its Best | Mary McNulty | 112 |
| Mistake In Afghanistan | Stephen Morse | 113 |
| Your Final Hours | Shirley Fordham | 114 |
| Transaction | David Hall | 115 |
| Sight, Sound And Sensation | Richard Styles | 116 |
| Great St Mary's Cambridge | Moira Clelland | 117 |
| Invading Our Territory | Beryl Johnson | 118 |
| An Angel At Dawn | Valerie Ann Knight | 119 |
| Knock And It Shall Be Opened Unto You | Pamela Willison | 120 |
| The 1886 Carousel | Louise King | 121 |
| Castor Hanglands | Pat Homer-Wooff | 122 |

| | | |
|---|---|---|
| Passing | Andrew Crump | 122 |
| Turn To The Lord | David Ashley Reddish | 123 |
| Stepping Stone | Pearl Cornwell | 123 |
| The Brick Yard | Margaret Cryer | 124 |
| Friends | Margaret Pay | 125 |
| The Gift Of Life | Joan Wright | 126 |
| Prayer For Here And Now | John Brackenbury | 126 |
| Untitled | Marina Yedigaroff | 127 |
| Black Hearted | Sharron Hollingsworth | 128 |
| The Queen's Jubilee | Robert Baslington | 129 |
| The Dark And Half Past | Antony Picking | 130 |
| My Shadow | Charlotte Gibbons | 130 |
| I Saw You | Nicola Grant | 131 |
| Cleatham, Lincolnshire | Dianne Roberts | 131 |
| Jim | Jodie McKane | 132 |
| Cambridge On The Move | Helen Walker | 132 |
| Ode To A Brother | Raymond Law | 133 |
| Lamp-Maid Jane's Poem Fruit Yields Around Nene River | Louis Don Barrow | 133 |
| The Great Floods | W Oliver | 134 |
| The World Is Wonderful | Julie Brown | 134 |
| Faith | Valerie Hewson | 135 |
| The Daisy | Mary E Calthrop | 136 |
| Llewellyn | Patricia Crouter | 136 |
| The Universe | Enid Hewitt | 137 |
| Down Memory Lane | Harry Skinn | 138 |
| My Destiny | Beryl Sylvia Rusmanis | 139 |
| Fun And Bloom | Elsie Moore | 140 |
| Welcome To Our Home | E Jones (Betty) | 140 |
| Bridge Over Troubled Water | Catherine Armstrong | 141 |
| Blackbirds Take To Wing | Polly Bennison | 142 |
| Untitled | Sophie Lianne Perkins | 142 |
| Thanks | Norma Spillett | 143 |
| New Experience | Dennis Bensley | 144 |
| Doubt Not | A R Barnes | 144 |
| Dawn Awakening | Carole King | 145 |

## TREADING ON DOLPHINS

Memories:
Fragments in time, floating
Like dandelion clocks in a current of air;
Settling like spare buttons in a jar
They clothe days sewn together
However untidily
Which unravel gradually
To become a patchwork
Of texture, senses
Held together by the mind, distilled;
Like crazy paving, or mosaic
Fitting together to form
A picture for time
To walk on
Like tourists at Herculaneum
Treading on dolphins.

*Fran Harris*


## UNTITLED

Whispers of justice, of anger, of youth,
Are wrapped up in echoes of unstated truth,
Where love wears an armour of silver and gold,
Outshining the army of glory untold,
Beneath all the beauty and glow of success,
Stand castles of glass from a heart of excess,
But higher than these glows the unceasing power,
Of the beautiful, honourable ivory tower.

*C Woolmore*

## STAMBOURNE

*As it was in the beginning*
Nestled deep in the countryside beside a stony stream,
Someone built a dwelling place, in which to sit and dream.
This dream became reality; and grew with rural power,
Till there were several cottages; and flintstone church with tower!
So the tiny village grew, to manifest a dream;
Of someone who had found a place beside a stony stream.

*Is now*
Tho' many centuries now have passed; the fields still grow their corn,
And there's a solace ever found, where wends the silver Bourne.
The church, her new-found strength displays; steadfast ticks her clock;
As blessings of her saints abide; and watches o'er her flock.

*And ever shall be*
Centuries come, and centuries go, but the green of grass and tree;
And the song of water o'er stones, pronounce eternity!
Cuddled in the arm of trees, the church remains serene;
And all because long time ago;
    Someone came to sit and dream!

*Patricia E Woodley*


## THE BAR IS A GARDEN

Is the bar a garden?
Then the bar person is a weed
To save you from the toil
Of everyone's everlasting greed.

Is the bar a garden?
Then the bar person is a weed
Who late at night hears your troubles
Then helps you with your needs.

Is the bar a garden?
Then the bar person is a weed
Who needs nothing from their side of the bar
Because of what they see.

*Keith L Powell*

## THE POWER OF NOW

Beneath the weeping willow tree,
There seems a force of destiny,
A sense of strength,
A cloud of gold,
Around a mystery untold.
Beneath a blanket on the ground,
There lies a question to abound,
A long lost tongue,
To answer all,
Deciphering beyond the call.
Beneath the rotting sediment,
Unfolds the history of descent,
A dormant thought,
A feeling strong,
Epitome of right and wrong.
Beneath the unearthed boundary,
We push aside sweet harmony,
We find ourselves,
In deep torment,
In search of lasting wonderment.
Beneath the sanctuary of sleep,
Befalls a past we must not keep,
Be rid, be free,
Just *now* remains,
To open heart, unleash the chains.

*Geraldine Sanders*

## Norfolk Grave

Looking from my window
The winter sun in brilliance beaming through
The yew tree in the churchyard
Still bedecked with morning dew
The hour was calm and peaceful
So clean and fresh the air
When within my sight a figure
Faltering in the graveyard there.

Unsteady steps he planted
Stooping low with stick in hand
And at heel his faithful collie
Till at last he came to stand -
By a headstone veiled in mossy fleece
And tilted in the ground.

My gaze I could not alter
But with reverence did I view
In his arms the freshest flowers
Of multi-tinted hue
His head now bowed and down his cheek
Without wincing or grimace
A gentle teardrop fell to earth
As sweet memories were retraced.

And then the faithful collie
Rose, shook its coat of white and black
Fondly nudged its master
It was time to saunter back
So when the two had gone away
Curiosity pressed my thought
I clambered up the old stone steps
Quite unknowing what I sought.

'To my dear parents' carved from old
The brief inscription read
'Lives well lived and lives well loved'
No more was need be said
I stood as if within a trance
And was constrained to bow the head
And whisper in the stillness
'May that too of us be read.'

Thank you for our three dear hearts
For all the joys and sorrows
Thanks for strength to guide and steer
And bless all of their tomorrows
Help us, ever help us,
To weave your wisdom with your grace
May we live well and well be loved
Memories sweet for them to trace.

*Trish Duxbury*


## MY CHILD

What is it to love,
Or to be loved?

It's a path that we all have followed,
Sometimes reaching the end and still feeling unfulfilled.
Then there is a love of a child,
A love that only a parent will know,
No chance of unfulfilment,
As their love is innocent and holds no conditions.
And what do we give in return?
Simply every beat of our heart,
Every breath that we take
And every moment in time.

*Tara Borg*

## A Lincolnshire Landscape

Within days the land that stood close locked
With golden, fat eared grain,
Glissanding in the breeze
Awaiting the harvester's attention,
Now lies close-cropped bristle,
Like the head of the new recruit.
Startled stalks stand stiffened,
The trees like newly exposed ears
Taut and bleak in the coldness.
Across the shortened stalks
Run multicoloured rainbows,
Fighting and dancing in the air,
Preening and walking proud headed
As pheasants stroll their turf.
In another field stand seagulls,
Positioned like so many chess pieces
On an invisible grid, each one alone,
Yet together they wait
Until knight jumps to king's bishop 4
And they wheel away raucously
In startled flight, only to return once more.
Yet again the eye shifts -
This time spying smoke
Rising in the still autumnal air
As rubbish from ditches and drains
Is burned away.
On the grey stoned wall
The virginia creeper blasts out a final trumpeting cry
In gold and red and orange,
Defiant against the onset of the winter season.
And children, poking high in the air,
Collect and peel away the spiked coats
Of conkers, ready for the fight.

Then comes home the cat
With dusty, day-tired paws,
Bearing a gift of feather or of shrew,
And settles before the fire
To clean whisker, paw and tail,
Before blissful purring announces -
'I am home. I am safe. I am here'.

***Una McLean-Manning***


# I CANNOT COPE

I cannot cope with war
I cannot cope with brutality
I cannot divine the core
    of the source of immortality

I cannot cope
I cannot cope with lies
I cannot cope with ties
    that are not profound
not mutually very sound
    adverse to my mentality

I cannot cope
I cannot cope with insolence
I cannot cope with violence
based on pure hostility
causing me incompatibility
being sheer futility

All those vices exist
seem to rule and persist
unless virtues will unite
enlighten men to be more bright . . .

***Wila Yagel***

## JANUARY MORNING

I venture forth to purchase bread,
While clouds are scudding overhead,
And gutters choked and wide, retain
The aftermath of recent rain.
But I, with anxious, skyward glance,
See signs of sun, and take my chance.
A frisky wind invades the town,
And drives the black umbrella down.

The doggy man at number two,
Calls out, 'Good morning, how are you?'
That red Capri at number five,
Is edging, cautious, from the drive.
I duly pause to let him go,
The pavement's clear. Along comes Jo.
Little and wise and seventy-three,
But when I stoop, she kisses me!

We bandy forth the latest news,
Then it's 'Goodbye, and mind those queues!'
That newsagents was full today,
But when there's bills, I like to pay.
That's how they taught us, long ago.
'Well, cheerio, take care,' says Jo.
She blows me kisses, merry-eyed,
And I walk on with lighter stride.

Contented now, with errands done,
I note with gladness how the sun,
Just as the weather girl foretold,
Is turning dampened streets to gold.
I slow my pace and turn my head,
To scan each garden flower bed.
On modest borders filled with light,
Near snowdrops blooms the aconite.

And I can dream of springtime hills,
And Billy Wordsmith's Daffodils.

*John Guy*


## THE HARBOUR MOUTH

What ships have sailed forth in years gone by
From countries and far off lands?
Crossed the oceans and weathered storms
Before they drew alongside your sands.
What cargo did they carry in the bellies of their hold?
What secrets did they keep never to unfold?
As they sailed into this harbour mouth
Bringing goods from foreign shores.
Who were they? Where did they come from?
I stand here to reflect and pause,
And think of time gone by, many years ago
The land has seen great changes,
But one thing of which I'm sure
The sea remains the same
As it holds these ships afloat,
And silently supports them
Mighty ships to tiny fishing boat.

*Sue Cooper*

## SAIL AWAY

Why ask me to justify my love of poetry?
Is it not clear to see,
The bliss it brings, the joy it brings,
The hope it brings to me?

O the elation of being swept away,
In this sea of a million words!
As it ebbs and flows my spirit grows
And shouts to make itself heard.

We poets will sail away together
And travel from land to land.
Across the sea in a vessel of unity,
We will make our own stand.

We can't promise love or happiness,
We can't promise that you will be saved.
But what is guaranteed is that you will be freed
By the gentle rhythm of the waves.

Words flow as freely as the water,
Be it over sand, ice or rock.
Barrier cliffs - my grief; forgiving beach - my relief,
As the seconds wash away on the eternal clock.

Every place on this green and blue orb
Is reached by these harmonious seas.
And like the vast oceans we will link the emotions
Of all nationalities.

So I will show you why poetry, to me,
Is the medium that I love the most;
Just disband your fears, use your eyes and your ears,
And take a trip to the coast . . .

*Jodie Bradshaw*

## What Did You Do In The War Daddy?

'What did you do in the war Daddy?'
Said a quiet little voice -
'What I did in the war Laddie
Was not anything to rejoice,
I saw young soldiers die Son,
Fear and hatred on their face
They were scared - but if they had run away
It would surely have been a disgrace.

The loved ones we left behind Son
Were brave, courageous and strong
They toiled - they worked - and they prayed Son
And hoped it would not last long.
The mothers, sisters, wives so dear
Sang to the children to ease their fears.
Friends were made, but not to last
Each day - another one going so fast.

All the killing, maiming and the tears
Plans were made - as months turned into years.
I have never understood why, Son,
We should have wars at all
Marching in rain and mud Son
Dodging the bombs when they fall
So - the things we did in the war Son
We will not linger upon.

So do not ask me - what I did Son,
Don't bring back the memories of yore
Let's put all of those horrors behind us
And pray for a world without war.'

*Jacqueline Ellen Boorman*

## My Garden

Now I am more housebound my garden is my chapel
Every morning I sit on a seat and pray
First I thank the Lord for another precious day
I walk through the rose arch down the aisle
The pansies are the congregation, they greet me with a smile
In the centre is a bird bath which looks just like a font
The birds all come to bathe and drink just what they want
Passion flowers read out the Scriptures of the crucifixion it is said
A crimson poppy droops its petals
And I remember loved ones that are dead
The delphiniums look like a choir, I can almost hear them singing
Foxgloves and Canterbury bells are also loudly ringing
London pride reminds me of the place where I was born
My signature are the daisies scattered on the lawn
A magpie is the vicar, preaching from the roof above
He is telling me to count my blessings and of the Saviour's love
I am very much enlightened as I walk back indoors
Knowing that God has given me strength to tackle my daily chores.

*Daisy Gilson*


## Observations From A Train Window

White hills stretching as far as the eye can see
Barren beauty unbroken save for some solitary tree
Here an ice pond frozen and some sheep in isolation
Stare silently at the stranger, sharing God's creation

Blue sky drapes over this desolate scene
Untouched, unspoiled, new, crisp, clean
I can taste the fresh beauty, feel the icy air
Encircle my very being, lay my soul bare

Weak winter sun casts shadows without warmth
Incapable of melting the ice in the trough
The field now lays fallow, no leaves on the tree
Yet rich is the beauty enveloping me.

*Edna D'Lima*


## TRYING TO KEEP HEALTHY

What are we supposed to eat to keep us healthy today?
You must eat plenty of vegetables so they say
When they put all those chemicals on the land to kill the weeds
It must get into the vegetables that we do need.
They tell us to eat meat but all those injections they put in the cows
It must affect the meat and also the flavour somehow,
Not like the meat we had in the good old days
When Mum cooked a leg of lamb, such a little to pay
They say if you eat fish it's good for you and me
Then they say it's contaminated by the pollution in the sea
So what are we going to eat to keep our bodies in trim?
If we do not eat these things our bodies will get too slim
We were always told bread is the staff of life
Now they say only eat the brown, there's no goodness in white.
Oh dear, it seems to get worse, what are we supposed to do?
They say all the food with 'E's is bad for you too
Then they say if you eat butter that causes a lot of fat
So if we eat margarine what do they put in that?
Eggs are not good if they are battery fed ones
They should be free range so the chickens have a good run.
Sugar and salt are bad, they say, can cause heart disease.
It seems worse and worse, I now begin to feel weak at the knees.
I think I'll now give up and do myself omelette and cheese
Then perhaps I can rest and settle and put my mind at ease.

*Olive Peck*

## THE RIGHT MOVE

I moved to East Anglia over eight years ago.
So, I would like to tell you why, I love it so.
In winter, it's a picture postcard scene,
In spring, the different shades of green,
The summer sun's a sheer delight,
And the orange skies we have at night.
Some of the views would take your breath away,
As there's no sky scrapers in the way.
The people here are friendly with a heart of gold
But, don't upset their way of living
Because you will be told,
Always respect the place where you live,
And you'll find it's got a lot to give.
I've lived in Epsom, Brighton
And good old Dorking town
But Norfolk is the place now
Where I have settled down.

*Sheila Buckingham*


## THROUGH KYLE'S EYES
*(Dedicated to Kyle Hobbs aged nine months)*

Don't just look and stare at me,
I'm a person not a disability.
To cast me off and think I can do nothing,
Is wrong, I'm not a teddy filled with stuffing.

I have feelings and thoughts just like you,
There isn't much that I can't do.
I may take longer to reach a goal,
But I do get there and with good control.

To talk down at me like I am thick,
Is an attitude that makes me sick.
I am living and have got a brain,
Down's syndrome doesn't make you insane.

So if you come across someone like me,
Go deep inside not just what you see.
It may even give you a great big surprise,
About this condition you'll become more wise.

*Elizabeth Farrow*

## A WINNER'S GAME

Fathers, mothers, sisters, brothers,
Triers, criers and deep chip pan fryers,
Writers, fighters,
Lonely daughters and overnight porters.
Sportsmen and women pursuing recreation,
Seek your compelling, good inspiration,
Seek the key to their salvation.
Please, let us receive the invitation.
Let us jump, let us sing,
Let us dance, let us shout,
Spreading the good news, 'God is about!'
Relay around the neighbourhood,
For no extra charge He'll make it good,
In fact He'll make no charge at all,
He'll even reverse a long distance call.
The line is open, waiting just for you,
The game has started; here is your cue;
Have a go; it's a winner's game,
Once you've tried it, you'll never feel the same.
It's great; it's great.
You'll feel young and free,
Even if you're aged 103!

*Julia McNeill*

## SMALL IS BEAUTIFUL

A tiny blue tit caught the eye
Its colour bright against a clear blue sky.
Feeding from a flowering shrub
Winter long, small yellow flowers bud.

Pure white snowdrops, their beauty rare
Arrive in the winter when the earth is bare.
Tiny white violets growing everywhere
Their wonderful perfume fills the air.

A newborn foal, a splendid sight
Jumping for joy in pure delight.
The perky robin on the fence
His breast a brilliant red.
Singing his wondrous song
As he waits to be fed.

A tortoiseshell butterfly unique and rare
Kaleidoscope colours and pattern fair.
The nectar-rich blooms of the buddleia flower
Prove irresistible as the shrubs colourful power.

Along the banks primroses are found
Every spring they never let us down.
An exquisite wren in a chestnut tree
Sings his song, strong and free.

A majestic moon lighting up the Earth
Twinkling stars shine for all they're worth.
A newbornbaby, in one's arms we hold
The miracle of life, a wonder to behold.

*Aves Swanson*

## In Summertime

I see before me lines of tums,
And cleavage of the workmen's bums,
Each neckline low to show more chest,
Than seen before at summer fest.

A little sun is all they need,
To show the skin that hides indeed,
Behind the modern clothing bright,
That grips their bodies very tight.

For once the sun is out all day,
Devotion to it, they have to pay,
And every inch of skin must be,
Available for that tan, you see.

They worship it with great devotion,
Lying, half naked by the ocean,
To catch the rays of harmful sun,
Which toast them like a currant bun?

If they don't pay the price of pain,
The tan is just a worthless gain,
They have to show it off to those,
Who don't divest themselves of clothes?

So this to me, is summertime?
When Brits go mad in weather fine,
To tone their skin from pink to brown,
Whilst holidaying, way out of town.

**Nigel Lloyd Maltby**

## INDEPENDENT WOMAN

Being a woman is so hard
It's demanding and daring at times
Always on the go,
Always having something on your mind.
Changing in so many ways
Not knowing what tomorrow brings
And if tomorrow will come
What is to be done?
So many things to do,
So many places to see,
Still doing the same things as
You did the day before.
Not finishing what you started
Not doing what you intended to do
Being an independent woman
Is hard for woman like me
And you.

*Emma Graham (17)*


## TUPHOLME ABBEY
*(Near Bardney, Lincolnshire)*

Tupholme Abbey had much to say
In days of glory, from stones yellow-grey.
The tumbling ruin, was once so loud
With triumphant praises from cloisters proud.

Sheep graze on covered hummocks, alone,
Where godly monks, working, used to roam.
And silent forever, the clanging bell,
That called them back to prayer and cell.

This holy ground, so loved long ago,
Which talked of heaven where all can go,
Stands half neglected, letting time pass.
It lies, isolated, lonely, given to grass.

But while no longer sending songs to the sky,
Its spirits lives on beside Witham banks high.
But not 'twix the arches of moss-tinted stones,
It lives among Christian churches and homes.

*David Radford*

## POWERFUL FORCES

Reluctant summer, overdue,
a welcome sight with skies of blue,
with sun streaming down from on high.
Then nature's great power lets fly,
sudden heavy torrential rain
spatters against the windowpane,
light breeze changes to gale force, fierce,
and jagged forks of lightning pierce
the rapidly darkening cloud.
Followed by rumbling noise, so loud,
comes the sound of thunder clashing,
the wild wind blowing and lashing
with abandoned fury, so fraught,
trees, contorted by the onslaught
twisting, tossing from side to side.
Creating havoc far and wide.
Loosened leaves, foliage shaken,
prematurely drop, forsaken,
strewn upon the ground far below.
And now the wind ceases to blow,
storm receding, birds start to sing,
the elements have had their fling.

*Lilian Owen*

## BELLS FOR THE BRIDGE

Red roses play concrete games,
Bruised and battered by the onset of autumn.
Cellulite petals pronounce them dead, announce the dropping
Parachutes shot from the sky - ashen
They fall for the dirt, canopies for the ants.

Wet mother will beat their heads in,
Concussed armour pinched and pincered
Rips the flesh, allowing for leaks in these shanty dwellings
Washing the soldiers away. Food for the gods.

Laudanum leaves shelter the lost
Moist warmth in the dew of dawn - contagious as our human beds
Until the prickling sticks of history's hand grope the garden mystery,
Fingering the worms from dark, dank tunnels
Blind as man and wriggling in half, as the shells grind them down.
The black and white photograph holds heroes - dusted down,
Strengthening the bridge as iron legs bound to a time
A ghost game that traffic cannot halt - continuous gunfire
Even as the flowers are laid.

*S P Springthorpe*


## MEMORIES

By the shores of Hunstanton together we stray.
Laughing and recalling joys of yesterday.
The peace and contentment we feel beside this shore
Reminds us of our childhood days so happy and secure.
So let us add this memory to the many that we share
For these are golden memories with which nothing can compare.

*Barbara King*

## ODE TO NORFOLK

Every morning I arise
And greet these wide East Anglian skies.
The dawn begins a pale cool light
Shrugging off the cloak of night
Birds their chorus long begun
Bid a welcome to the sun.

Rushes whisper to the reeds
Telling secrets no one heeds
Poppies scarlet, fragile, sway
Hiding in the fields all day
Peeping out amid the corn
Shyly greet the coming dawn.

Towering cliffs and Broadlands fair.
Marshes, home to creatures rare
Contrasts of the land and sea
Ever changing, ever free.
Shingles clatter with the tides
Solitude, and peace abides.

Hidden creek, stately home,
Sweeping sands the sea to comb.
Windmills, sails, boats and people,
Leafy lane and old church steeple
Glorious sunsets end the day
A fiery red and pink display.

Night enfolds us in her arms
Her canopy above us calms
A million stars like jewels peep
And give us comfort while we sleep,
The moon shines bright, so old and wise
As if to guard East Anglian skies.

**Beryl D Graham**

## KING'S LYNN - OLD AND NEW
*(Written in 1975)*

King's Lynn is a town, of quiet renown,
It has charms both old and new,
When once you've been there, you begin to care,
It has a close hold on you.

By the River Ouse, folk ponder and muse,
Is it flowing out or in?
What a splendid sight, as a bird takes flight,
It's gliding towards West Lynn.

The ferry sails past, often it's a hard task.
To struggle against the tide,
It then turns around, fills with people bound,
For 'Lynn' on the other side.

Tuesday Market Place, full of serene grace,
When it is tranquil and still,
But on market day, in noisy 'affray',
Folk can buy and sell at will.

There's no traffic now, it's replaced somehow,
With many a paving stone,
They look very nice, but cost such a price,
You heard the rate-payers moan.

St Margaret's Church, from its holy perch,
Looks serenely down below,
Should you be in doubt, the clock will point out,
If it's time to come or go.

The new indoor pool, will help keep us cool,
When life's at a hectic pace,
Museum of old, now stands proud and bold,
That too now holds a new face.

Buses now turn round, on different ground,
A new bus office, of course,
New shopping precinct, modern and distinct,
With seats everywhere to pause.

New flats look downstreet, on the old Millfleet,
Aged library still stands there,
Red Mount looks around, from high on its mound,
It can guard the walks with care.

Give King's Lynn her due, she blends in the new,
And still her old charms remain,
Let's not count the cost, for once these are lost,
They're not easy to regain.

**Kathy Jordan**



## LET'S DANCE

Come let's join the dance.
We may be old.
Time has left its mark
But let's join the dance
And be young again.
By chance,
They played our tune.
We smiled, and started
To remember
The way we used to dance,
Slowly, held close.
We closed our eyes,
We were young again
Celebrating that wedding day
Fifty years ago.

**Anne Hornigold**

## DANGEROUS GIFT

I am the crackle of wood,
The sudden explosion of light,
The transformation of the atmosphere.

I am the presence that cheers or appals,
That brings gifts to man
Or takes away his possessions.

I bring gaiety to the simple home,
Leaping and sparkling in my strength ever-new,
And people crowd around to worship me.

I am the overhauler of forests,
The liberator of dormant seed,
The life-bringing Angel of Death.

I am the restlessness beneath the earth's crust,
The mover of buildings,
The force that must escape.

I turn mountains inside out
And gush upon the ocean floor;
I dance for joy on the face of the sun.

I am the ultimate purifier,
The creator of art and industry,
Improbably transmuting.

I am the symbol of love and hate:
I make tender hearts to race,
But punish countries with war and tumult.

I am often the servant of men,
But never entirely their slave,
For my power is too great.

Make use of my arts in all their diversity,
But treat me with discretion,
Or you will regret it.

*Fire*

**Anne Sanderson**

## THE VIOLINIST

When watching the recital, in St Nicholas' Church,
With piano and violin, my heart gave a lurch,
For the beautiful music, given to me,
A vision that only my eyes could see.

Right close to the violinist, a spiritual figure there,
And I could only sit and stare,
A figure in a cloak and hood,
It must be Him, I knew it would.

I could feel His strength and I could tell,
It was for the violinist, who'd been feeling unwell,
As the magical music filled the air,
The spirit of Jesus was standing there.

What a wonderful sight, it was to see,
My heart felt it had been set free,
My little story, I had to tell,
But I didn't explain it very well.

Perhaps I could have told it a little more,
As I left the musician and made for the door,
But I think he was happy and he knew,
That Jesus was there, beside him too.

**Winifred Booth**

## A Hand To Hold

A hand to hold, and a shoulder to cry on -
That's what Christ means to me.
A harbour to bring my poor boat safely into
When I'm tossed on life's stormy sea.

A light to lighten my darkness
When I'm travelling on a pitch-black road;
Someone to tell all my troubles to
When I'm carrying a much too heavy load.

A hand to hold, and someone to rely on -
That's what Christ means to me.

My peace in a world filled with trouble;
My comfort when I'm suffering pain;
My refuge when trials surround me,
My *joy* - for He brings sunshine after rain!

A hand to hold. one I'll always depend on -
That's what Christ means to me.

*G Walklett*


## The Warm Glow

That first conscious thought, as night turns to day
Confusion? Too soon for the sun, or even first light,
Then recognition, it came from within.
I know too well, the bubbling, outpouring fire when we touch,
Fuelled by the giving, and taking, and sharing,
But this 'warm glow' you've given me,
Becoming familiar,
Still surprises me, as each new day breaks.

*Erica Sillett*

## PASSING THROUGH

Dark clouds of deep despair loom up upon life's brightness like a storm
The distant thunder rolls, and echoes thoughts within the fevered brain
While overhead the clouds swirl round and tear apart and then reform
And with the scalding tears comes down the heavy torrent of the rain
These falling tears now slowly ease and cease to flow at last
A wind of calm blows fresh and soft to move the storm clouds by.
The muddy waters flow away to join the river of the past
And now the sky turns blue and clear, a balm that quells the heavy sigh
The flowers glisten in the clear clean air like jewels in a crown
The birds emerge from every tree to preen their feathers in the sun
The world begins to smile, as from his orbit he looks brightly down
To light the road to hope and laughter, a new era has begun.

*A J Spencer*


## WHY?

Two little lives taken away,
Just as they were enjoying their day,
Two little mites whose lives had just begun.
I hope who did this, will be surely hung
Or they ought to be, for causing such grief
And robbing parents of happiness, is beyond my belief.
Holly and Jessica you are away from more harm
But *why* were they taken without qualm?
All the lovely flowers from people who care
And the love that emanates for all to share
Is surely a lift to the parents' hearts,
To know they are not alone, but from all parts
People are praying and sending their love,
It doesn't bring them back, but looked after with God above.

God bless them all.

*E Harrod*

## REGRETS

I've loved for pleasure
Made it my leisure.
I've loved in haste
Curious for a brief, sweet taste.
I've loved in vain
Perversely hoping it would make me sane.
I've loved and taken many a thing
Charmed, seduced, been treated like a king -
I've received so much that I could burst
Yet still have such a raging thirst.

I've loved with finite, desperate hope.
Loved for money - gone down that slippery slope.
Many times I loved myself more than others -
Cast blame on all the future mothers -
Who give without thinking of receiving
So now I'm all alone and grieving -
For I missed the point of love itself -
Missed its richness and its wealth.
I've received so much that I could burst -
Yet to truly live, I must start loving first.

*C B Walklett*


## THE SLIPPER CHAPEL

The heavy wooden door stood ajar
Cool tiles beneath our feet
Warmth from the lighted candles filled the air
Flames flickering in the breeze
This perfect place of paradise so peaceful and serene
A time for reflection with a wish it would last forever
But life goes on.

*Olive Poole*

## At Season's Close

There's a kind
And quiet
Softness
As the summer
Passes on.
Our fields of grain
Lay waiting,
Having dried
By scorching
Sun.
Mellow mists
Of autumn,
Change horizons
From far
To near.
And gentle stillness
Whispers,
With a hint
Of skylark
Song.
There's peace,
Tranquillity,
Beauty,
As far
As one's eyes
Can see.
The landscape
Of the Fens,
From here
To
Eternity.

**Lyn Sandford**

## BLACKBIRD DITTY

Mr Blackbird is a fighter,
Patrols his 'patch' with glee,
Stands with wings akimbo
Patrols his territory.
Takes on all 'newcomers'
And wins that day, at least,
Tours around the garden
For foe who come to feast.

He has a yellow eye-ring
With dapper bill to match -
His feathers black and ruffled,
His stance upright to watch.
He's the first to arrive for breakfast
The last to retire at night -
The pluckiest little 'gamecock'
Always ready for a fight.

His wife wears a smart brown outfit
With accessories to match,
She arrives later for breakfast
(Mr B gets the early-worm catch!)
She's an expert homestead builder -
Secures the nest with mud,
Incubates eggs with affection
And then expects help from 'Dad'.

When the chicks are fat and fluffy
They stand and wait for food -
Open their gapes quite widely
For beetles and worms that taste good.
They're tucked away each evening
And sung to every night,
But when Mr B wakes the next morning
It's time for another fight!

*Pam Dutton*

## SOUND BECOMES SILENCE

Everything is alive
but not everyone can choose:
we connect sound
to the motion of living,
our racial souls
sing to be free.

Yet another exile
of voices beyond the sea:
the music of war
and we are dancers
trooping the death march.

There were children
in Treblinka
    the choir of Orpheus:
in Belsen you feel
their bodies moving.

The future is talking
word upon word
but no-one listens
or witnesses our tears.

Perhaps we will not see
the saints pour their song
from Heaven and heal
our choral rage.

Learning to be kind
returning ashes to flesh
must sound become silence
    will the Earth only grow wise
in the absence of singing?

**Simon Richardson**

## IN MY DREAMS

In my dreams!
I hold you close
And trace your beauty
Allowing the warmth of your body
To melt my heart

In my dreams!
The softness of your skin
And that sparkle within
Mixes a magic potion
That floats me into paradise

In my dreams!
I can chase through your mind
And unlock that passion
You hide, deep inside

In my dreams!
I run my fingers
Through your silken hair
Showing you
How much I care

In my dreams!
I hold your hand
And walk you
Through the golden sand
Where we watch the moonlight
Kiss the rippling waves

In my dreams!
I am in Heaven
With you 'my angel!'
By my side.

In my dreams!
You love me!

*David Duthie*


## LOOKING AT A DEAD MAN'S THINGS

Like a peculiar garage sale, his charred possessions
spread across the lawn, tempting a browser.
She watches men bring out armchairs,
singed covers flapping in the sooty breeze.

They struggle with the mattress
and its pool of fireman's water.
She pictures him in bed when it started,
his head on one side, smoke stealing into his nose.

Her eager body leans over the low, neat hedge,
to nudge at cabinet doors.
Inside a perfect row of dead man's shoes,
ten pairs, polished, reachable.

She holds her bag tight on the bus,
hides her bargain from other passengers.
When she gets there, her father makes tea
so pleased to see his generous daughter.

She scrapes soot from her fingernails,
drops it discreetly on his kitchen floor
while he tunes in the radio, dances for her,
laughing at the taps of his new, brown brogues.

*Rebecca Goss*

## A Beautiful Place

In my mind a beautiful place is what I see
A place which has no cruelty
A place which is meant for you and me.

A place where there's no hunger, homelessness or sadness
A place full of joy and gladness

Where love and laughter is spread all around
A love that is so silent it doesn't make a sound

What a better and happier place this would be
For now and all eternity.

*Suzanne Reeves*


## A Word Of Advice?

List *it*,
Twist *it*,
Take *it* apart and fix *it*.
Love *it*,
Leave *it*,
Trust *it* to your arms
Deceive *it*.
Take *it*,
Make *it*,
Put a smile on your face
and fake *it*.
Pull *it*,
Push *it*,
Rip *it* up and forget *it*.
Take *it* with a pinch of salt.

*H B Walklett*

## DELIRIUM

I saw visions on the ceiling,
A strange cat was on my bed,
I heard a voice, as through a haze,
'Don't get too near,' it said,
I was wandering through different rooms,
Searching for my own
But nothing was familiar,
I felt so all alone.
Something wet was on my face
Was something drowning me?
I tried to swim, I couldn't move,
My legs flailed helplessly,
I floated then, up to the clouds,
Some angels passed me by,
Was I now in Heaven,
Did I really die?

But then, I was back down again
Still looking for my room
Unfamiliar faces
Peered at me through the gloom,
Panic overtook me
I had to get back home,
The voice that shouted 'Help me,'
Must have been my own.
Suddenly I felt quite calm
My eyes were open wide,
I was back again in the room I knew,
With great relief, I cried.
'Where have I been?' I asked my mum,
As she gently mopped my brow,
'You've had the fever,' she replied,
'But you'll soon be better now!'

*D Morgan*

## Pictures In The Fire

Quick-cold, from the swirling moorland mist,
I embraced the crackling fire,
Deep in the flames as the green logs hissed,
I watched the years expire.
At first the horse drawn carriage came,
The old queen laid inside,
It leapt from the depths of the red hot flame
Then dematerialised.

Outside the window darkness draped
Her all embracing shroud,
Then out of the fire a sound escaped
A screaming starving crowd.
Their famished faces flesh on bone,
Like yellow stones on sand,
Beside the Thames, a resplendent dome,
Towered over fertile land.

The fire replenished, glass in hand
I focused once again,
There were women making strong demands,
In purple, white and green,
Women marching, heads held high,
Huge hats with ostrich plumes,
'Votes for women' was their cry,
But a blinkered battle loomed.

The flames receded, embers glowed,
The wind had settled down.
And in the warmth white crosses showed,
The millions underground.
And high above a canopy,
The deathly parasol,
In all its glowing panoply
A holocaustic pall.

My room was cast in darkening shade,
The hearth a gentle red,
Through the city streets, a cavalcade
Was winding, like a thread.
The gun carriage moved through the sobbing crowd,
And an era neared its end,
As Elton's voice rang clear and loud
'A Candle In The Wind'.

*Pat Coldwell*


## THOSE WERE THE DAYS

Among a myriad of thoughts recalled from the past
Nearly all of them fleeting and not meant to last
Are memories of girl friends now vanished and gone
Like those ships in the night or an echoing song

At a prep school for children first Margaret I met
Then followed Iris and Phyllis and almost a set
Of Joan's in succession total number was four
Plus Dinks, Daphne, Dorothy to push up the score

Later came Thelma and Lilian and then just prior to war
A new Margaret and Phyllis with more memories to store
Though Eunice and Edna both hold a place I still find
Fond thoughts of Eileen and Gwen can still jog my mind

No doubt there are others whose names I've forgot
To remind me of days and when I should probably not
Relive old memories when we hoped youth would last
Using rose-tinted spectacles and those thoughts of the past!

Plus Uncle Tom Cobley an' all!

*M F Base*

## ESSEX

I travelled out from London,
On the Central Line.
Left the train at Ongar,
No lighter heart than mine.

Planned to roam round Essex,
Survey the rural scene.
Take in all its hamlets,
View each village green.

Searching for the peasant life,
Seeking relics of the past.
Sleeping at old coaching inns,
Ploughman's lunches for repast.

I strolled down leafy lanes,
Through village and through glade.
Prayed in forgotten churches,
Whose bells in silence stayed.

Rambled through country churchyards,
Whose headstones, local names recall.
The late yeomanry of Essex,
Landowners great and small.

Before I set out on my journey,
They said, 'Now fancy that,
Who'd want to visit Essex
It's dreary and it's flat.'

Well! Forget Southend and Clacton,
And stuffy Frinton by the Sea.
See Finchingfield so beautiful,
Great Baddow or Tiptree.

Speak names like Epping Upland,
Steeple Bumstead and Marks Tay.
The Higher and Lesser Rodings,
Laver de la Haye.

Saw picturesque thatched cottages
Large windmills now at rest.
A rich and verdant countryside
By Mother Nature blest.

*John Bracken*


## PRAYER FOR EAST ANGLIA

Lord may we in East Anglia see you face to face
May we know the power of your saving grace
Show to us your glory and splendour we pray
And lead us along life's way

Let your river of life flow among us
As we look unto Jesus
The name that is above every other name
Past, present and future always the same

Thank you for giving us your son
And forgive the sins we have done
Send your holy spirit from above
And embrace us with your pure love

Lord please hear our cry
And do not pass us by
Grant to us our greatest desire Lord
And set this region on fire for Jesus, your living word!

*Carl Waite*

## Untitled

'Oh, the light at the end of the tunnel.'
How often these words are said,
When fear overtakes as a runnel,
Negativity o'er runs our head.
But, this light at the end of the tunnel,
Is a spark or a glimmer divine.
A smile, from the odd passing stranger
Or, a handshake, quite firm, clasping mine.
There's a light at the end of the tunnel,
For those who are sad and bereaved.
And a word, or an ear, or an offer of help,
It's amazing what can be achieved.
So, our light at the end of a tunnel,
And the source, when the light is in view,
Is not really that odd,
It's a gift, yes from God,
A 'lighthouse', for just me, and you.

*Lew Park*


## Snowflakes

A snowflake melts when you grasp it.
It dissolves and leaves you with nothing to hold.
Snowflakes are delicate and blow on the winds,
Hold me and I'll stay here for as long as I can,
For I may be delicate, but I've been here too.
And when the wind blows, I'll be here for you.

*Gordon Finlay*

## IN MY NORFOLK - THE SOUND OF MUSIC

A sunny afternoon of peaceful quietness
When - flash - across the sky a jet is flying high.
This is *noise*
A field of golden corn where field mice romp and play.
The combine crashes in, its engine causes din.
This is *noise*
A sky of darkening clouds, the moon begins to hide
The lightning flashes high and thunder shakes the sky.
This is *noise*
The sands are empty now; no children laugh and shout.
The waves are foaming high, the seagulls shriek and cry.
This is *noise*
And then at break of morn the birds begin to stir,
Their chorus fills the air, the lark sings sweet and clear.
This is *music.*

*E Barker*


## ROBERT

I know a boy called Robert who means a lot to me,
He's eight years old, with a heart of gold,
And he stands as straight as a tree.
He's a footballer, a trumpeter, and he sang in the choir too.
He reads very well, can write and spell, and he'll do anything for you.
He's a sensitive lad, loves his mum and dad,
And his brother too, most of the time.
It's easy to see why he means so much to me,
This wonderful grandson of mine.

*Jacqueline Hartnett*

## THE INVISIBLE CORD

Joined by a cord - that can never be seen.
Attached by the spirit that stays evergreen.
Fused together as one, in thought and in mind
in a love that is special, truly one of a kind.

As a babe on my knee, he could never do wrong
I would hold him so close, so soft, yet so strong.
Then a young boy at school, he was so quick to learn,
soon a man he would be and a wage he would earn.

As a lad in his teens - he would then play the field,
I watched him with care and my heavy heart reeled.
For I knew I could lose him, too soon and too fast,
but the love that I had for him always would last.

Not a day, not an hour, nor a minute goes by
when I don't think about him - or ask myself why,
should the cord (though unseen) that binds us, be shorn,
as the one that was cut, on the day he was born?

Then a wife he would pick and would choose to be wed
and I can't face the doubts that come into my head.
Would he be a provider - as his father before?
Would he give all he had - 'til he could give no more?

In his steel-blue eyes, as he looks fondly at me
and the depths into which only I can see
is the truth and the hurt and the sorrow inside
for the times that he failed and the times that he tried.

When his own children came and they sat on his knee,
did he think or remember his sessions with me?
He will raise them with love, such as only he can,
now at last the cord's snapped - my son is a man!

*Maureen Ayling*

## Hadleigh Castle

Once the proud sentinel of the Thames' mouth,
Its great walls in desolate ruin lie;
This Norman built guardian of the south,
Now razed and open to the Essex sky.

From the Benfleet heights it scanned the sea lane
With an ever vigilant scrutiny,
Beyond the estuary, out to the main
It searched for invasion and mutiny.

What human effort was here expended,
What a scene of health and mind-wrecking toil!
So territory could be defended -
This newly captured prize of English soil.

More than a century it took to build.
Father, son and grandson, all laboured here;
To the conqueror's will all had to yield,
When menaced by the sword and constant fear.

So many resources were spent in vain,
For these walls never heard war's din and blast;
No land-hungry aggressor ever came,
The Norman Conquest was this island's last.

Part of the south-east tower still remains,
Looming over where land and water meet,
Scowling down on noisy, model-like trains,
That dart between Southend and Fenchurch Street.

Nature decrees that all things must decay,
Even stone castles, like men, run their race;
Cruel time has stolen almost all away,
Leaving this a wounded, melancholy place.

*Arthur Allen*

## THE NEXT MORNING

Reaching out my hand
I touch a leg.
It is not mine, I know
because I have checked.
Looking over my shoulder I see a body,
thankfully asleep.

Can I remember last night?

Easing myself slowly out of the bed,
I tiptoe into the bathroom.
Looking in the mirror,
causes a surprise
too much to drink again,
just look at those eyes.

Splashing water on my face
as I sit on the edge of the bath.
Gripping the sink
aching for a drink.
Back in the bedroom
I gather my clothes.

Slowly dressing, I stumble against a chair,
a voice asks sleepily, 'Are you there?'
With some hesitation I turn
trying not to scare,
'You're up early,'
said my wife.

*Paul Kelly*

## MEMORIES

Memories are those shadowy things,
That appear, then fade away.
They fill our minds for a second,
And we cannot make them stay.

They hide inside a world so vast,
Of thoughts and things we know.
These wispy trails of magic,
Feel free to come and go.

And when we choose to concentrate,
To put our thoughts on track,
They flash across our waiting minds,
And the instances come back.

Our heads are full of where and when,
And how and what and who.
But without these moody memories,
We haven't got a clue.

They are the masters, there's no doubt,
So if you want a memory out,
Just hope today they're at their best,
And let imagination do the rest.

Memories are those shadowy things,
That appear then fade away.
For information, fingers crossed,
And hope that they will stay.

*Duchess Newman*

## Yesterday's Child

My mind is like a picture book,
Full of things at which to look.
Where I recall my hopes and fears,
And my dreams of childhood years.

When life seemed clear as black and white,
Good and bad, wrong or right.
And that's how it would always stay,
With no awkward shades of grey.

But now the child is fully grown,
And from the nest this bird has flown.
But how I wish in some small way,
To be that child of yesterday.

**Helen T Westley**


## Night Of The Full Moon

The stillness of a moonlit night
When all the land is bathed in light.
In woodlands images appear
As moonlight shines through the trees.
Awesome, weird . . . a feel of fear;
An owl hoots in the distance . . .
Creatures of the night appear.
On roads and streets
Of towns and cities
The moon casts shadows
In all its glories.
There's magic and beauty;
A clarity . . . and peace
Permeates the air.

**H S Persse**

# A Question Of Poetry

What do you do when you
dry up and find that you're lacking
in inspiration - pull at the roots of your
hair, expire from frustration, climb the walls
live on your head, rant, rave and roar, or go quiet
to your bed? Do you get out and interact with the
wide world around you or feel just like Shelley
and scream - 'I wanna drown too.'
Or . . . do you dive into your favourite
Keatsian
ode, coughing
profoundly, yet
profusely, feeling
little better than
a toad. Do you feel
the need to be rid of
these cruel shores and
take off for better
climes abroad,
where one day
perhaps your
name will be;
writ on water
for all eternity.
. . . or will your
epitaph
just read:
'charlatan'
and 'fraud'?

Do you live, sleep and dream
poesy all of your life, how
often does it caress you, how
often cut like a knife?

*Rosiane Walklett*

## WHITEOUT

Set off early in the morning to cover all the miles.
Cold and misty at ground level, but then the ground did rise.
Moving up, my legs grew weary, weighed down, overworked.
Fingers reddened, just as threatening as the snow that lurked.
Yet through the wall, the mountain lake, the distinct path beyond,
Descending under rain clouds onto road and village fond,
Pausing briefly to recover and mend my feet of pride,
But the stormy track soon vanished under the whiteout sky.
Everyone was going down, the other way from me,
Not just ambling, but as if there was something to flee.

Still, amidst the grey-soaked air the path stayed visible,
Yet the higher and the colder, the more the pale dust fell,
Until there was no path to see and just a compass map,
To counter weather, to find the way, reappearing track,
To counter losing any hope and filling my safety sack,
To stop the rescue team coming out to carry my body back.
From hope came panic, conflicting plans, book without line-links.
Following fence lines, what I thought were human signs, footprints,
Knowing I was foolish. No one knew my route. No one.
Forgot that I was watched and kept alive by someone.

Sudden inspiration - this wall goes to a high peak then stops,
So if I follow it then turn and walk east I will not here drop,
So off I run and make the turn and utter prayers to be led forth.
Suddenly meet a pair of walkers who confirm that I am lost.
Yet they point the way ahead and tell me to avoid the cliff
And soon I'm heading safe away, towards my home beneath the mist.
I'm tempted to congratulate myself on saving me from fate
But where did the skill come from? And I could have been walking late
And missed the pair and got the darkness,
Wandering round in bedlam weight.
I could have fallen down a slope or been blown down away forever.
Someone was looking out for me. He didn't see it as time for Heaven.

*Andrew Sanders*

## I'VE LOST MY DOG
*(Hannah, German Shepherd 1977-1989)*

There is a pain within my heart
It cannot ever leave me
A heavy sadness I must bare
And why? 'Cause Hannah's died
You see -

This tearful grief, my sobbing heart
I've lost my dearest friend.
My darling Hannah's died
You see -
Her life has reached its end.

Through 12 short years I loved her so
Her love I never doubted
A place within my life was hers
Her presence always counted.
I don't know what to do,
You see -
My heart it can't recover, a special love I had for her
That's touched me as no other.

I visit where she rests in peace
I kneel close to the ground
I place my hands upon the soil
In sorrow I could drown
And yet she offers up to me
A comfort pure and true
She can no longer be with me
But you see -
Hannah I pray, that one day
I'll be with you.

***Judith Hill***

## SUFFER LITTLE CHILDREN
*(Dedicated to the memory of Holly and Jessica)*

The world shares with you sorrow and grief
Traumatised by disbelief.
Two girls murdered, discarded in dust
Driven by man's perversion and insatiable lust.

Cold by the stories we constantly hear
All parents now shall exist in eternal fear
Watching each movement and act of their child
Waiting in hope that they are not abducted and defiled.

All we require is police on the beat
To protect them the innocent from betrayal or deceit
Those who are in charge, to pass relevant laws
Not to listen, then rapidly close the door.

We live with the memories and honour the dead
But those girls should be alive and asleep in their beds
Although we are many, we now stand as one
Act now we implore, before another child's gone.

Suffer little children were the words Christ did preach
But killing, perversion he did not beseech
Open your eyes, now is the time
To live and to cherish but act wisely against crime.

For while we allow these people the freedom they seek
There will be no place for the feeble and weak
For the victims, there needs to be justice that's fair
Stand up and show that we are a nation that cares.

*Lynda Fordham*

## HAND IN HAND

Marriage is a partnership
Where two become as one;
But do not wait until too late
To think 'What have I done?'

Your lives are joined together,
So you may agree
On every little thing in life
In total harmony.

If there seems to be a time
When you are in doubt,
Talk it over with each other,
Discuss what it's about.

Giving your life to Jesus Christ
Is just the same you know!
You must walk hand in hand with him
Wherever you may go.

Tell him all your troubles,
Give him all your cares;
Be in fellowship with him,
In all things let him share.

Your heart and hands entwine with his
For you must work together.
Walk steadfastly towards the goal;
Christ's love endures for ever.

***Christine Lemon***

## A Very English Summer

We were many miles east
Of the smoke choked beast,
Diamonds crushed to coals
By the pitiless pressure,
Storm in store for sure,
Raven clouds hovered overhead
Obscuring the egg-yolk glow of the day.
He sat before me, not just breathing
But truly feeling the summery sauna-steam
As it burrowed its way into purging lungs.

They shot the lame horses here,
He told me.

The first tears fell heavily,
Thumping the butterscotch grass
Defiling the parched chalky earth.
Below us the dust creaked as it guzzled.

When they were useless,
He continued.

Streaming now, arrows from above
Biting the ground around us,
Punching the sweat from our scalps,
Fingering our faces with random prods.

All I need is a rope and a favour,
He begged.

The bark of the malformed tree
Was greasy and glassy
From the downpour.
Branches glistened like slugs.

No noose is good news.
He laughed.

We waited for the rain to pass,
Driving home past the glue works.
It was a nice day for it.

*Jon Oyster*


## Cherish Your Childhood

Who is the lost boy
With the wide eyes and
The lungs that could
Laugh for all time?

Why do I cry?

What is the sum
Of his dreams at
The hour of one
In his life?

Should I reach out?

How can his senses
Resist all the new
And the glimmer
And shape of these things?

Can I see?

Where will he stop
To reflect on the
Past that was one
Short-lived dream -

'What ails the old man?'

*Graeme Vine*

## THE PATH OF LIFE

Life's path is full of twists and turns;
So many ways to go.
A baby falls, and quickly learns
Some choices turn to woe.
As children progress through the years,
More vistas come in view;
The onset now of hopes and fears -
Which pathway to pursue?

The caring parents try to lead
Along a steady path,
But young ones very seldom heed -
Life should be one long laugh.
Some take the trendy 'get rich' trail
And care not how they travel;
But when their health begins to fail
They wish life could unravel.

Others turn to drugs and drink
For a life of 'highs and lows';
They have to find how far they sink
To prove one reaps as sows.
Help is at hand for you to take
If you find it hard to decide.
The right decision you can make
If you let God be your guide.

Reach out in faith and trust His word;
He waits for you to ask.
Be strong, and do not be deterred,
He'll equip you for the task.
Go forward then, and do your best,
Life's race will soon be run.
And when God calls you to your rest
You'll hear Him say, 'Well done'.

*Joan Picton*

## FOREVER LOVE

When I think of you a tear drops down from my eye,
And joins my love in the ocean of affection and happiness
Which you have made flow from a mere trickle, deep in my heart.
You have thread your love and compassion
And sewn up all of my hatred and fear,
Mending my pain with your strength.
You have turned dim light into burning flames of joy,
Blankets of thorns into quilts of roses
For my body to lie on and strengthen.
My heart deepens and my joy flows out
And showers my life like silver droplets
Raining down from the gods in high Heaven
Bringing hope to the whole world,
Bringing hope and happiness,
Joy to my soul, love to my heart
For the rest of my life,
Forever.

***Kate Long***


## FEELING

If I can see you, then you exist,
If my heart skips a beat, then I can feel you.
If my mind is filled with pictures of you
Then I know you are somewhere.
At the dawning of the day,
When my heart is weighted
I can look up to the sky, and see you.
When the light is shut out
There is a hope
That remains undistinguished.

***Joanna Smith***

## 1953

It all happened in 1953
The crowning of Elizabeth, our queen to be,
And folk were waiting the great celebration
That was due to be shown on BBC television!
Such fairytale scenes our eyes would behold,
The streets would almost be paved with gold;'
We wanted to see this great panorama
But were expecting a different kind of drama.

Our baby was due on this special day
So we hoped to be off without further delay,
All poised and ready for the great event
But our baby was too comfortable and content;
Alas! There would be no hint of distraction
Or cause for alarm at a first contraction,
No! 'Twasn't the time to be bringing us cheer
Or even to pick up a coronation souvenir.

Excitement mounted as each day passed
And the moment of joy had come at last,
God's precious gift - a wonderful sight,
A girl this time, oh, what sheer delight,
The boys both came to look in the cot
And Peter said, 'How many feet's she got?'
Once we were two - but now we are three,
Thank you God for a lovely family.

*Beryl Sigournay*


## LIFE

Life is a blessing from above
It comes with the swiftness of a turtle dove
Every time a child is born
It comes as swiftly as the coming morn

As the sun's first rays hit the world
A ball opens up that has long since been curled
A child has been born oh what a treasure
To live a life full of pure pleasure.

*Racheal Shanks (13)*

## HOME COUNTIES ESSEX SOUTH EAST

The glacier headed for Yarmouth e'er life had its dawn
It struck poor Walton on its Naze e'er history was born.
It flattened all before it, 300 feet it towers,
Before they had a football team, it met defeat at Bowers!
There had been ice before it; far greater cold it knew,
It must have done, even the clay it left behind is blue!
'Second' left yellow clay, ten feet thick it lay,
If you dig deep you find it today, and Essex is known for clay.
You can get bogged down in the stuff as I am doing now;
But the first glacier covered France,
The next stopped here - by chance?
No: a marsh that was hot! It stopped at that spot.
The answer, a gulf far away
Where the water boiled over and poured out a stream
That sought for a cold place to dream.
So far, far away it ventured one day, a stream that encountered a stream
In imprisonment harsh - it was lost in a marsh,
And the gulf stream its ice fetters broke.
The two waters met and are doing so yet, or we'd freeze here,
each year, until March.
'Get back to basics' they say. Well these are our basics today.
I could tell you lots more, but I don't want to bore.
Although there is plenty to say. Do you go far away
Where 'the past's' on display, for each year's holiday?
Well try Essex - 2003.

*E Norman*

## IN THE FUTURE?

The world is at peace,
Our planet is safe
There is now a future,
For the whole human race,
The weapons have gone,
That killed and harmed,
For all nations
Have at last dis-armed.
*The world has calmed.*

Freezing from the cold
Is a thing of the past,
Our heat comes from nature
And it lasts and lasts.
The sea and the wind
Are our friends it seems,
As the fires in our homes
Glitter and gleam.
*The sun and the moon - brighter beams.*

Starvation has gone
Throughout the globe
And no one goes
Without any clothes.
The people of the world
Now do care
That everyone
Gets, their fair share.
*And no one is bare.*

Every human now
Has a place to dwell,
There is no longer a need,
To buy and sell,
Rogue landlords
Have bitten the dust,
All rents now,
Are fair and just.
*Housing was a must.*

Fish are abundant
In the sea
It is safe to swim there
For you and me
The oceans, rivers
And the sea
Are as clear as crystal,
And pollution free.
*No pollution was the key.*

Birds are happy
Up in the sky,
Being free from danger,
To hover and fly,
For they are no longer
Shot, just for a game,
Or, caught by humans,
Just to tame.
*Preservation was the name.*

Oh! What a dream
This would be,
A wonderful 2003
For all to see
And to give the children,
Yet to be born,
Hope for the future,
With every new dawn,
*The line in the sand has been drawn.*

**S B Kershaw**




## ANTICIPATING SUMMER

You gave me life again
Which I had lost then
Autumn was, yet spring sprang
From your heart and I sang

Winter is over and done
Now, sunshine looks shyly down;
Moodily, showers show how
Hard it is an hour to know

You would I love ever
More, whatever the weather;
Were I a paid-out plummet,
Measure steadily to summer

***Barnaby Lockyer***

## SWIMMING IN THE MUD

Did I tell you the time,
When the weather was fine?
We went down to the seaside to swim.
We jumped on our bikes,
Got a terrible fright,
When we got there, the sea wasn't in!

At Southend-on-Sea,
This is how things can be,
When the tide's out, there's nothing but mud.
But we wanted to swim
So we waded right in,
And fell on our butts with a thud!

There was mud everywhere,
From our feet to our hair,
And it smelt of pongy-poo fish.
But my daughter who's seven
Was in seventh heaven
To be covered in mud was her wish!

So next time you go
Be in the know,
Check out the times of the tide.
But who really cares?
With mud everywhere,
We were having the times of our lives!

**Katherine Lunn**

## DESENSITISED

What would life be for me without sight?
Eternal deception within dark depths of night
I could no longer discern the beauty of creation
existence - blind mystery - confusion without cessation
I would be lost to all colours in a jungle of monochrome
and everyday - a white stick battleground, in and out of home.

But more than this if I was unable to see
I could no longer gaze upon your radiance, whilst next to me.

If I was to have taken from me all sense of smell
all atmospheres would seem the same, what could I tell
about a person, a danger, an area or food?
Flowers would become pointless, bitter and crude
life would become near tasteless too by implication
no aromatic awareness - the death of nasal sensation.

But severest of all, if I was deprived of this sense
I could only smell your glorious hair and skin in the past tense.

If I should wake no longer to hear,
unaided by sound, my speech too unclear
I could no longer be transfixed by the calm sound of a
                                                      creature's content
and would be open to all the dangers this noiseless world sent.
I could no longer judge by emphasis or tone of voice
and would be imprisoned in a musicless void with little
                                                      reason to rejoice.
But over and above all these things I would lose
I would mourn most the loss of your sweet promises - loving muse.

It would be indescribable to lose the sense of touch
such a primal pleasure, vital emotional crutch
for it's this sense that tells us that the others are real -
the ability to comfort becomes the miracle to heal.
Administered with love it's simply the greatest gift
capable of curing the harshest words, deeds - the deepest rifts.

But most crucially, if I no longer possessed the sense to feel
holding you would be like an hallucination - just unreal.

If the ability to taste should disappear from within me
my palate would dry out, my glands would envy.
A paralysis would set in from my lips to my parched throat
food would give no satisfaction, yet my stomach would bloat
out of an intense yearning to relish and savour
lush cooling liquid, life's bitter sweet flavour.

But worst of all, if this sense should desert my mouth
I could no longer taste you while kissing you - from north to south.

If I was to lose the sixth sense - that elusive indescribable thing
that we call instinct, intuition, feeling
I could not sense moods, opportunity or danger any longer
I would become weaker, yet my will naively stronger
with no sense of control over myself or those around me
I would slip, fall overboard and drown in an emotionless sea.

But best of all if my sixth sense was no longer to be
I could rest content, unaware that one day soon you'll leave me.

*Lorna Walklett*

## THE STORY OF LIFE

Life is like a story, it begins, it also ends
Nobody knows the outcome, on events it just depends.
For some their life is holy, for some their life is fun
For some the story ends even before it has begun
No index to show where you're going or what you're meant to do
The course the adventure takes you on is mostly up to you
For some the story gets tedious, they choose to end it quick
Others thrive on life, their volumes get forever thick
Lives make interesting reading, telling tales of wealth or glory
Others barely fill a page for there's no meaning to their story
Some stories are young, some stories are old
Some stories are secret, some long to be told
Some books can show the caring, some others can destroy
Some chapters filled with tragedy and others filled with joy
Some lives full of many chapters, others not quite so long
Some lives published perfectly, others published wrong
Some books may be hard to take, some seem boring or distraught
Others seem informative where a lesson may be taught
Some have stories too good to be true
Others seem like they've happened to you.
Your story can be the best or worst that you make it
The volume depends on the journey you take it
For some the journey's cut quite short, for some it's a bed of roses
For some of us it's still being written, so now the chapter closes . . .

*Darren Ferguson*

## THE BUNGALOW

The hallway yawned black;
A pale face appeared:
A well-etched life map.
A freckled hand bore an
Empty milk bottle
To place, shakily, on the doorstep.
The yawning black swallowed the half figure
In one gulp.

Like an over-sized ominous beetle
The black vehicle
Shuddered in the kerb.
Sloe-black dressed men:
Two in number, emerged to
Disappear, temporarily,
In the same, yawning, hallway.

There's a 'For Sale' sign
In the weedy garden
Of the bungalow: No 3 Melbray Avenue;
The roses have wilted;
Fingers of sunlight
Probe the lace curtains
And gain entry
But there is no one there to warm.
A 'For Sale' sign is taken down in Heaven.

***Joy Lennick***

## Adoption

You did not grow within my womb
Nor suckle at my breast.
But in a shabby crowded room
I choose you above the rest.

I did not give you blood of mine
Or my genes to you impart.
But when you looked and smiled at me
I then gave you my heart.

I never felt the pain of birth.
That agony so sweet.
But as I saw you lying there
Our bonding was complete.

You may not be blood of my blood
But you are the only one
To take my heart and make it yours.
My chosen precious son.

*Pamela Matthews*


## Out Of The Blue

Out of the blue
Comes the new
Illumined One,
Bright as the sun.
Brother of the poor.
Peace not war.
For evermore.
He comes to you,
Out of the blue.

*U Johnson*

## THE BEACH

Soft, wet footprints disturb the purple sheen,
summer sandals swing at your fingertips,
discarded shirt flaps loosely on your hips
and lapping waves wash all your sadness clean.
I walk behind, careful, less I offend
the tranquillity that's come to you this day
and whisper to the wind 'Why must this end?'

Pausing I hear the swooping seabirds call
reminding me that sea and sand stay on,
reeds and grasses sing their summer song.
Now I am old, I have no doubt at all
that love will last even though I must die
and other footsteps will caress this sand,
new lovers face the sun and question why.

*John Talman*


## WHY?

Why is the sea so cold and blue?
Why the spring grass fresh, and new?
Why is the sky so dark at night?
Why is snow so pure, and white?
Why storm clouds black and swirling blue?
Why mist leaves damp and dusky hue?
Why the wind so cold it blows?
Why does Jack Frost freeze our toes?
Why is each day so unsure?
Yet, as time passes our love grows more!

*Trina Mayes*

## MOBILE LOVESONG

Hi Babes! I'm here at Waterloo
The train's been cancelled - there's a queue
But I just had to talk to you
Just had to say I love you.

Hi Babes! Kiss kiss! I'm on a train
Two hours delay - it's pouring rain
But I just had to phone again,
Just had to say I love you.

I like the way you've ironed my jeans -
Those creases you've put in the seams
Babes, you're the girl in all my dreams -
Just had to say I love you.

Hello again - yes thanks I'm fine -
But leaves are falling on the line
Won't make that interview in time -
Oh Babes, just say 'I love you'.

Some geezer's kicking up a fuss -
He wants to put us on a bus
Those falling leaves are stoppin' us
Oh Babes, please say 'I love you'.

Hi there Babes! This is no joke!
I'm on a bus for Basingstoke
Sat on my mobile - something broke -
Ju . . . ha . . . t . . . sa . . . I love y . . .

*J Oliver*

## FLAMES OF LOVE

Two candles burning
In the dark
Lit by two souls
Now far apart
A token of love
One for the other
A silent prayer
To a faraway lover.

The flames shine out
Strong and true
A beacon from the heart
Their vows to renew
Smoke curls to Heaven
And meets way up high
Uniting their love
In the deep blue sky

They feel the connection
Though still far apart
Sweet reassurance
Swells their hearts
Warm contented feelings
Flood each the same
And in mind and soul
They're together again.

*Janet Mills*

## MUSIC OF THE MIND

Do you want to hear music?
Then listen, for it's over and under and there
Wherever you want to find it,
It will hover in the air?

You'll hear music in dawn-song chorus
And also a baby's first cry.
You'll hear it again in the evening
When day begins to die.

It will come to you in a moment
When you lover calls your name
And you'll hear it when least expected,
Always new and yet ever the same.

It's the sound of a kettle boiling
When you're thirsty and very tired.
There's music of crackling greenwood
When you're resting beside the fire.

As the wind blows across the meadows
In the sound of an Aeolian harp;
Sometimes the notes will be gentle,
Still others vibrating and sharp.

But just as your eyelids are closing
And you leave the day's worries behind.
The wonderful music of silence
Will be heard in the depths of your mind.

*Catherine May*

## THE COURT OF OWLS

Beneath my feet
Sleep the priors,
In this court of owls
Their priory has become.

Bell tongues
And owl songs
Collide above the marsh.
Faintly, by the river,
Plainsong adds a tenor.

I linger here,
Hearing not listening,
My mind upon distant things.

Could they rise,
What would they say,
What would they sing?
Ave, alleluia?

Our angel,
Outstretched over all,
Folds me to her breast
And I rise with the owlbells,
Invisible among the brothers.

And we sing . . .

*Richard Maslen*

# TIME

Time is a clock that goes on and on
It will never stop for you, me or anyone
You might not think of the years that lie ahead
Or for the amount of time you spend in your bed
For when you are young time doesn't count at all
As life in general is one big ball
You don't even worry or stress, you just enjoy your life
Then as you grow older you get a husband or wife
Time then seems to fly like blinking your eye
Just as quick as the clouds change in the sky
A family you then have and you watch them grow
Then one day you look in the mirror and it does show
For time has aged you, it says it all on your face
And it happens to us all in every race
No matter what your faith, religion or colour of your skin
Time is a factor that no one can win
So enjoy your life, be happy, keep safe and well
For time is moving on and it will surely tell
For you may wish one day that you had done more
As time will run out and that's for sure.

*V M Seaman*


# IF

If we all were insects,
And buzzed around in flowers and trees
Would humans then be great big giants?
And would we bang into their knees?

If there were no humans
And the world were ruled by pigs or hogs
Would they have religious thoughts?
And would there be such things as gods?

If there were no monkeys,
And the brightest things were toads and frogs
Then when it started raining,
Would it still rain cats and dogs?

But if there were no life on Earth
And empty seas stood ten feet tall
Would there be need of you or me?
Or anything exist, at all?

*Richard Lee Nettleton*


## CENTIPEDE IN THE SKY

I saw a centipede in the sky,
As aircraft, unseen passing by
Leeched out its far off vapour trail;
And one, I feel, could not fail
To marvel at this distinctive sight,
From vantage point toward fast approaching night;
And in imaginings, as would ancient man,
How such a phenomena as this began,
No reason came that would suffice,
Other than sign, or heavenly device;
And still this centipede progressed,
Progressed cross-sky toward fast fading west;
And as it feathered cross the sky,
Its vapour trails dissipating by and by -
I saw it as a sign, some ancient text,
That we are but at very best,
A fleeting message written high,
As this brief encounter in the sky.

*Jean Rosemary Regan*

## QUESTIONS AND ANSWERS

When you know all the answers, you know all there is to know.
When you've been to all the places, you've seen all there is to show.
But will you ever understand the workings of a brain,
Driven to the edge and barely crawling back again?

It's easy in your perfect world to sit with peace of mind,
But some of us don't live that way, perhaps we both are blind.
Perhaps we never can accept that all of us must differ,
And always in the wilderness, a lonely soul must shiver.

For time alone may heal the wound but always leaves the mark,
A reminder of the point in life when brilliance lit the dark.
When all the pain came welling up and thundered in your head,
Leaving dreams of solitude and wishing you were dead.

I don't suppose you comprehend an abstract point of view,
Suggesting all that you call fact is in fact untrue.
That love is pain and pain is love and those below are those above,
That lies insist that we believe all the lies that we receive.

For when you know all the answers, you know all there is to know.
When you've been to all the places, you've seen all there is to show.
But will you ever understand the workings of a brain,
Driven to the edge and barely crawling back again?

*Farrell & Wright*

## CHILTON BROOK, HUNDON, SUFFOLK

We are lucky to have
or though some people would not agree
a stream run through our village
on its way towards the sea.

Some people use it like a tip
but if only they could see
when tended and enhanced
the beauty it could be.

When in the floods it rises
it's a different picture entirely
it's wild, it's strong,
it rushes along rapidly.

There are fish and kingfishers
we only have to look
so people of Hundon
take pride in Chilton Brook.

*Yvonne Elizabeth Hicks*

## WINTER

Winter, when the evening shadows
In the afternoon do fall,
Winter, when the heavy coats
Are hanging in the hall.

The time when well lit windows
Send you hurrying up the path,
To reach the brightly glowing fire,
That draws you to the hearth.

Outside, the trees now naked,
Stand dormant, as they wait
For spring, who will in glory
Through winter's shadows break.

Shadows, hiding from us
Mother Nature's secret toil,
As fast she works, through winter months,
Her magic in the soil.

Her magic, by God's hand, is done
Before the winter's end,
And life in root and tree awakes,
To welcome spring again . . .

*Joan Hammond*

## SOVEREIGN OF THE SKY

Seagull flying high, king of the aqua sky,
Seagull flying low, searching to and fro,
Seagull on the ground, strutting with no sound,
Seagull cries out loud, piercing the white cloud,
Seagull glides with ease, upon the gentle breeze,
Seagull sovereign of the sea, looks down and laughs at me,
Seagull what a life you have, flying oh so free.

Seagull looks down upon the Earth, he's filled with humour,
                                                      glee and mirth,
Seagull laughs at human life, filled with problems, sadness and strife,
Seagull is happy, for he is free, he is protected by the ship's lee,
Seagull is strong he can fly against the storm, he can find
shelter secure and warm,
Seagull is vulnerable, for he can be hurt, by toxic pollution
                                                      and man-made dirt,
Seagull sovereign of the sea, looks down and laughs at me,
Seagull what a life you have flying oh so free.
Seagull your home is being destroyed, your precious
                                              domain may soon be void,
Seagull in the sea fish are dying, I can hear that you are crying,
Seagull your freedom is under review, by the danger that
                                                          we humans do,
Seagull cry out, for you need aid, to help right the wrongs
                                                    we humans have made,
Seagull dies of poison, pollution, he was too late to find a solution,
Seagull once sovereign of the sea looks down in anger at me,
Seagull what a life you once had flying oh so free.

*Corinda Daw*

## THE ACCIDENT

Went down to the local shops,
Needed taties, bread and chops.
Mooched around like shoppers do,
Then I thought I'd have a brew.

But my plans went all kaput,
'Cause I fell and broke my foot.
It looked, like a horror scene,
It's not the best I've ever been.

I could see my little car,
And 60 yards ain't very far.
Crawling with a muted moan,
In that crowd, I was alone.

Perhaps I looked like Wine'o Lil,
Because their actions rated nil.
I heaved along, the progress slow,
Another 40 yards to go.

Somehow I climbed into the car,
The whole affair was so bizarre.
My automatic buggy,
Took me right back home.

Now I'm in the hospital,
And can't get out to roam.
Next time I go shopping,
I'll walk all slow and prim.

It's amazing how much trouble,
One granny can get in.

*Duchess Newman*

## My Norfolk

Norfolk is the place to be,
With its miles of broads and sand and sea.
Historically it's second to none,
Lord Nelson is Norfolk's famous son.

The village of Caister is home to me,
A fishing community it used to be.
Our lifeboat men, courage never lack,
Their motto 'They Never Turn Back'.

Great Yarmouth is the town next door,
A popular resort, and what is more,
Famous for its bloaters and kippers,
Enjoyed by holiday makers and trippers.

Visit Norwich City, for you will find
Interests of a different kind.
The castle proud and cathedral fair,
Its ancient market in the open air.

I hope this potted history
Will tempt you to come to see
What Norfolk has to offer you,
Just waiting, for all to view.

*Helen Lock*

## A Helping Hand

A father said to his son one day
Now listen Son to what I say
In this world we are not all the same
There are the rich, the poor, the sick and the lame

There are those who grieve for loved ones gone
And the old folk who can't carry on
There are the homeless with nowhere to go
And the outcasts nobody wants to know

Remember my son these poor souls you'll see
Were once the same as you and me
The reason they have fallen low
Is that fate has dealt them a cruel blow

Have compassion for those less than you
Be sincere in all you do
Give them all the help you can
For this you will be a better man.

*H Willmott*


## DONKEY FRIENDS

One is brown, one is grey,
They always find the time to bray,
When Sidney comes with a sugar lump,
They give the garden gate a bump
To say don't keep us waiting here so long
Or we will break into a song
That can be heard a mile away
And wake the village up today.
Martha is greedy loves her food
Daisy stands - she seems to brood
On her life so long ago
When she was then neglected so.
A score plus years has she lived on Earth
No fancy prices is she worth.
She likes to be ridden, Martha as well,
A lovely green meadow is where they dwell
Stable large filled with straw
When it's really wet I shut the door
The life of Riley do they live
But pleasure to many have they give
They are both mine and I really care
For Daisy and Martha the donkey pair.

*Mary Rose*

## SPECIAL MOMENTS

In every fleeting moment
There are seconds ticking by
Wasted are the minutes
Hours turning into days with a sigh
But in every special moment
As you listen to a clock's ticking sound
There are lots of things happening in the world around
Every second! There are surgeons, doctors, nurses -
Who have lives to save
Women giving birth - what a joy!
Also people dying, going to their grave,
Accidents are happening, races are being won
Divorces are finalised
While others are just having fun
Some are tying the knot in loving wedded bliss
Others are enjoying the magic of their very first kiss
There are people in hunger, homeless
People that are in poverty, - poor
So make the most of what you have
And give a little bit more
Treasure every moment, every minute of your life
Never go to bed before solving an argument
Say you're sorry! Don't let your problems get rife!
As you never know just how many moments you will have
Make the most of them, try and fulfil your dreams
Face the world - be brave!
Otherwise your special moments could be lost in a twinkling of an eye
And before you know it, your life could have just passed you by.

*Michelle Luetchford*

## AN EASTERN PROMISE?

I shall never remove myself from East Anglia
Although I may travel to a warmer clime
There's natural beauty, quiet and historic
Many memories are with me all of the time.

In bareness of winter, tranquil the waterscape
Everything is dormant secluded and lazy
In summer it's different, another picture
Hot-sticky afternoons. Mornings mist-hazy.

From North Norfolk coastline (always bitterly cold)
As Arctic winds bring ice-laden weather
To Fenland, Broads, marshes and reed-beds
And Thetford's great forest, accompanied by heather.

Cambridgeshire is wonderful. Ely especially
(A daughter born in the hospital there)
Antiquated hamlets. The Hemingford's splendour
But Suffolk's the spot. Let me die where . . .

Bird song creates a romantic aura
Skylark's hovering is beyond any endeavour
Picturesque landscape. Dark productive earth
It's a pity we humans can't live here forever.

It may be flat but I like its magnificence.
Storm clouds approach making atmosphere angrier
Although I may travel to a warmer clime
I will never remove myself from East Anglia.

*John E Day*

## DIALOGUE

The man from Human Resources
Stepped briskly on to the dais.
His eyes were sharp and remorseless
As he met the workers' gaze.

Scraping his chair as he fixed on his foe,
The shop steward got to his feet
'There's something up and we want to know -
We don't want no deceit.'

'Economies of scale are what's needed,
Staffing-levels must be downsized.
We're advancing a dialogue,' HR pleaded,
'Production must be centralised.'

'What you have told us is nothin',
My members are left out in the cold.
You just keep jawin' and puffin'
And we feel as 'ow we've been sold.'

'We're monitoring natural wastage
To minimise losses of staff.
The scenario which we now face is,
Restructuring' - HR said with a laugh.

'It's funny for you, that's as may be -
You're tellin' us nothin' o' course,
An' we're left a-holdin' the baby
While you tricks the whole workforce.'

'We've launched a raft of measures
To progress cessation of production.
The company genuinely treasures
Staff loyalty since its induction.'

'Have us got our pay at the end of the week?
Ain't that what it's all about?
What with rafts and cessations to hear you speak
My members are fair worn out.'

'Production will cease, that's what we must face.
Redundancy Counsellors soon will explain.
Appropriate measures will then be in place
For your seamless departure without pain.'

**Rosemary Harvey**


# DEAR GRANDPA

You were the best Grandpa
You meant so much to me.
I hope you're looking down on us
I hope it's not hard to see.

They were the bestest times together
The Science Museum the most.
We had a lot of jokes together
Even when I would boast.

Every Tuesday night
You took me to Cubs.
You bought me my uniform
Is there anyone else I could love?

I know you love your grandchildren
Luke, Megan and Sam.
You are the greatest grandpa
And I'm your greatest fan.

**Luke Blurton (8)**

## Message To A PE Teacher
*(For Steven)*

What kind of man is he?
The man who chooses to teach PE,
A natural player who is good at games,
An asset to any team, winning always his aim,
I look at you and I want to please,
Even if it means filthy clothes and bleeding knees,
But I am not good at sports it's not easy,
I am not good even though I want to be,
I run, I try but I am never quite there,
My legs, hands and head to act together is rare,

The day for rugby is drawing near,
I lay in bed sick and full of fear,
Not of the match, that I can do,
Not of the others but Sir of you!
To be told you behave like a girl by a man you admire,
Leaves me empty inside with a face red as fire,
I really try, I really do,
But Sir I am just not like you,
I have never been chosen, although I am keen,
It's been hard to be the one nobody wants on the team,
Then to have an adult like you mocking me when I try,
You see Sir *I am a man because outside I don't cry,*
You give permission with your cutting words,
For the others to follow like an animal herd,

But wait, you will be old when I am a man,
You will be vulnerable the way that I am,
I will remember well what I have been taught,
That it is OK to bully someone different in action or thought,
Your snide remarks may not make a man of me,
But it will certainly make me hate all forms of PE.

*Pamela Morton*

## Husband, Dad And Friend

Throughout your life you meant so much to everyone you knew
A happy, wonderful family man who loved us all so true
Your friendship was unbounded, your warmth a joy to feel
Your parting brings such sorrow; family love will help it heal.

The precious woman left behind feels pain deep down inside
But those who are so close to her will comfort her with pride
Our family love was born from you
It strengthens through the years
The thought of you now somewhere safe will stem the flood of tears

When you first met your 'Janet' you didn't have a clue
That you had found your soulmate, and she had found hers too.
You worshipped one another as lovers and as friends
A love like that's eternal and never, ever ends

When you became our father, you took the role with pride
First came Sian and Sarah, then Dave, your son arrived
You nurtured, loved and taught us the difference 'tween right
and wrong
A part of you is part of us, so you live on so strong

You then became a grampa, to Luke and Meg and Sam
You passed your knowledge on to them, like only Grampa can
The picnics, and the holidays, the jokes and kisses too
These all make Grampa Blurton, yes Dad they all make you!

Good times outweigh the hard times
Great memories stay so strong
You'll be with us in all our thoughts, for eternity, that's years to come
The pain and heartache will subside; the sense of loss we hope will end
You are and always will be
An amazing husband, dad and friend.

*Siân Blurton*

## THE RED INTRUDER
*(On a visit to Essex University)*

Ah, red robin with your puffed out breast
Like some mighty feathered Pavarotti
Today you sang a song of such piercing sweetness
Up there in a naked birch among those dark towers of learning
I saw you, with needle pointed beak thrust skywards,
Sing with the fervour of an evangelical crusader
Your message burst forth on the alien landscape
Whilst scarf-clad students scurried by,
Late for lectures, late for lunchtime pizzas,
Half finished essays flapping white-winged in disorder.
How they stared when they saw me transfixed on the pathway.
Silly old woman, silly old thing!
But they did not hear that lone robin sing . . .

*Sylvia Horder*


## LOVE POETRY

Should I possess
all the words in the world,
I might write something
worth the view;
a dictionary of love, perhaps,
purely meant for you.
But mad invention, amorous fun,
is surely not for us.
No need for terms between we two,
when the simplest words will do
    simply being, I love you.

*Paul Divine*

## VISITORS

Some may come
And some may go,
And some go on forever
Or so it seems.

The family come bounding in
I love to see them come
They bring their friends and more beside.
They like their breakfast nicely fried.
The washer drier does its job
The kettle's always on the hob.
From every room goes up the cry
'Mum do you know where is my . . . ?'
They disappear into the night
And come back when the day is bright
And then they go.

I like my visitors to be
Thankful for a cup of tea.
Early to bed and late to rise -
Philosophical and wise
Who make their stay not overlong
And never find their hostess wrong.

Tho' perhaps this is a trifle hard
The family have all been barred
But tomorrow is another day
There'll be no change I hope and pray!

*Margaret Adams*

## ATTICS OF MY HEART

There's a labyrinth of alleys
Filled with moments of my life
From soft and warming pillows
To a cutting table knife
Down passages and turnings
I race from or race to
For all I've met, or yet to come
I remember each of you

There are streets which have an absence
Without end and without start
I climb as lighthouse keeper
To the attics of my heart

For all the golden memories
Which spring from what we share
In solitude and reverence
I replay life with care
With peace and one affection
Retrace life anew
Combine my pleasure keeping
With quiet thoughts of you

There are stairs forever climbing
Without end or without start
I sail as lighthouse keeper
To the attics of my heart

Cold cavities of motion
I laugh, I cry, I blush
Still life painted on canvas
By the hand of old time's brush
For these moments that I treasure
Which I alone may know
Where I keep the strings of life
Untangle as I go

Down coalmines, to the vaults of mind
To my gallery of Art
My beginnings and ends are stored
In the attics of my heart

*Robin E Edwards*


## NORFOLK RETREATS

At Barton Mills the gateway to peace
closes behind me. Lest anyone find the key,
I pause good and long before I release
this news to you. But you know already
of Sandringham and the Broads. But have you
been to Gimingham, Squallm and Thrigby?
Will you ever find Lower Penn or Salle,
Titchwell Tower or Itteringham, Trunch too?

If you ask a Norfolk man, he will stall
by giving you squit with his best-laid-on drawl
in which he will say 'Don't go that way!'
We well may be safe here in Anmer and Holme -
despite that other Henge we've wot of for
yonks, like that petrified forest far out to sea -

so you grockles come now and search for the homes
where we hide; if you come, we'll up and bide
a while in marshes and sea-lavender, 'neath
lark call and heron wing, in high gorse and heath
ways Hardy'd have savoured. Vikings tried;
you too may though rather more peacefully
we've come to believe. So welcome ye other
folk and when you must leave us don't bother
to shut that gate; we'll lock it behind yew!
Our Norfolk pools be peaceful cum ye or noow.

*John Coleridge*

## THE COUNTRY BUS COMEDIANS

If it's plenty of laughter you are after,
With a happy smile for every mile
Then the Saturday fare to Market Square
Is worth every penny of your money

The bus is due and we are in the queue
Standing at the stop by the village shop
The bus time tables are just like fables
Believe them at your peril laughed Mrs Meryll

Here it comes said one of the mums
As the bus squealed to a halt with a familiar jolt
Amid diesel fumes and smoky plumes
We climbed aboard and the engine roared

The seats on the bus cause no end of fuss
Folk at the front must bear the brunt
Of folk at the back who just want to yak
As they turn round and say their news of the day

Next stop is the village pub, our centre and the hub
On gets farmer Giles all wreathed in smiles
He's full of cheer from all that beer
And jokes to the driver about change for a fiver

On gets Mrs Maggs clutching all sorts of bags
Her once blonde hair dyed black as soot
She boasted that her son's grown another foot
Of which she was pleased but doomed to be teased

Up chortled Mr Brown the resident clown
And retorted that the lad had got it sorted
For whatever the pace he'd win a three-legged race
And couldn't resist adding 'hands down'.

Don't just sit and stare, we're at Market Square
When it's time to alight there's an amusing sight
As those getting on push past the crowd getting off
Says the driver 'That's your lift, it's end of shift.'

**D M Harvey**


## THE GOLDEN JUBILEE

On Jubilee Day we partied all day,
With all our friends across the way,
Buntings flying in the street,
My it was a grand old treat,
Tables lined up in a row,
We dined and wined with friends and foe
Hunky firemen helping out,
'Come and get it' they all shout,
Pots and pans full of fare,
Oh what a banquet we did share,
Helping hands all around
Doing a damn good job we found,
Children in wonder enjoying the scene.
Is it real or is it a dream?
Tea was a treat, so much to eat,
Wobbly jellies served around
By hunky firemen I'll be bound!
God bless you all and Lizzie too
For helping us to see
The Jubilee through.
Roll on ten more years we pray
We wish you well, we really do
And then oh dear you never can tell?
We will party again
Along with you.

**Sue Vince**

## DANCE THE VIENNESE WALTZ

Dance the Viennese waltz
whirl to the music box
bodies grafted
swirling through the rising mist
heads falling back
in easy laughter.

Dance
dance
after wine
in the late summer
eyes locked
in a trance
and as you turn
figures on a wedding cake
the camera fixes
your china smiles.

Dance
your golden dance
spin like
fallen leaves
on a river.

Dance the dance
you must
her dress lifting
to brush
the watching shadows.

Peacocks
dream high in scented trees
under a crescent moon
and squirrels
fly with flashing eyes
and tails bright
with sparks
to guide
your manic feet.

Dance dance
till you drop.

*Colin Shaw*



## HOTEL STUDY

It stands alone as if by choice
with its once white emulsioned walls
now stained with green damp patches
that fan out as if dropped onto a piece of blotting paper.
The windows are grey and vague in clarity
threads of lace curtains half cover some of the windows
like a dead man left with half closed eyes.
Old hoarding appear through the weather
beaten surface of the facade like rare cave paintings
being discovered in an unpromising location;
an element of surprise that in this brick and
mortar collage is a blaze of colour;
however out of context or conviction
still exists as if that last good memory of times
gone by.

*Laurence D E Calvert*

## MISSING

In the midst of a happy family life
Comes suddenly an unbelievably awful day
There have been no rows, no quarrels or strife
But suddenly a much loved child has gone away
Endless thoughts race through the parent's mind
Has some stranger seized the vulnerable child?
Did they have a secret friend - desperate for clues to find
All sorts of possibilities, some terrible and wild
Keep one awake during night after sleepless night
First feeling hopeful, then in the depths of despair
Surely with so much help everything is bound to come right
Neighbours and family support you and show how much they care
You try to carry on, you must shop, eat and drink
Life for the rest of the family must somehow go on
But yet awful images crowd the mind, you try not to think
That without any goodbyes the loved one is gone
The mind is filled with memories and action replay
If only you could turn back the clock again
If you could hold the lost one there is so much you would say
Oh for an end to the torture of uncertainty and pain
Day after day goes by and it's the not knowing
That tortures the mind, waiting for the call
The child might come through the door, happy and glowing
Or be lying in a lonely grave, covered with soil
For some there will be a happy ending after all
Just a little adventure, embarked on without thought
Too busy with their own plans to make a call
Not realising how desperately they were being sought

*Margaret Meagher*

## AN EYE FOR AN EYE

What if an eye for an eye?
Then soon you would die.
Attack and counterattack
Until one cracks.
Unwilling and unneeded,
Unhappy and unheeded.
Go on and defy,
Don't dare to lie,
Don't give an eye for an eye.

What if an eye for an eye?
Then only your soul will fly.
One strong blow countered by another
Until one wounded will not bother.
Unloving and uncaring,
Unyielding and unsparing.
Go on and clarify,
Don't be scared to try,
Don't give an eye for an eye.

What if an eye for an eye?
Then only your worst will magnify.
Avenge and revenge
Until one flees rather than challenge.
Unwanted and unneeded
Unloved and unheeded.
Go on and try,
Don't justify,
Don't give an eye for an eye.

*Jocelyn Benham*

## SOUTHWOLD

A seaside resort on a winter afternoon.
Brooding. Watchful. Lifeless and cold.
It is closed, and resentful, grey and comatose.
Awaiting the return of the colourful, noisy masses,
To give it life, and voice, and joy again.

The sad, lustreless amusement arcades locked and dull,
No children wasting pocket money and grating on parents nerves.
The beaches are naked and vulnerable, stripped of their human cargo.
The streets and markets are empty,
No one selling, no one buying, no one shouting.

The winter breeze shunts litter in front of it like an invisible broom
Sweeping it under the carpet of the rain
The skies are leaden and uncomfortable, threatening all
The sky a shade of gunmetal grey which dares you outside
Without your umbrella. Go on, make my day.

A few people huddle on the seafront, hunched into the biting wind
Their faces saying - see, we are enjoying!
We prefer it like this - when it belongs to us alone
Their body language denies their expression,
Saying let's go! Home to warmth, a cup of tea.
Antiques Roadshow is on soon.

We'll come back in the summer, and laugh at the tourists,
And grumble at the sticky ice cream covered streets,
And deplore the flashing lights and the sound of slot
machines and sirens,
But at least it will be warm. And joyous, and tacky, and full of life.
But for now, the town waits, and sleeps, and dreams.

*Alison Housden*

## A Grandmother's Thoughts

A crying baby in your arms,
relaxed with body heavy,
fingers curled around your thumb,
she's sleepy, warm and steady.

An infant resting on your lap,
who smiles into your eyes,
and reaches up to touch your face,
a blessing in disguise.

A child of two or maybe three
sitting on the floor,
laughs with joy and raises arms,
as you wander through the door.

To play on the beach with a boy of eight,
in and out of the sea,
digging a hole as the tide comes in
and ruins it all with glee!

A girl of 12 with bright blue eyes,
a mother in the making,
who laughs and chats about the boys,
as she helps you with the baking.

How lucky I have been it seems
to have known and loved so well,
all these treasured memories
before the teenage hell!

***Pat Hayward***

## SET ME FREE

When you dropped me after all those years
My heart was broken, couldn't see for tears.
When you took your love away,
Felt, I couldn't face another day.
But when I got up this morning, the sun lit up the sky,
Felt so much happier, not going to let life pass me by.
Oh yes, I miss the closeness, the feeling someone is there,
But I am worth much more, you closed the door,
                                  you did not truly care.
Today a handsome stranger smiled at me in the street,
Made me feel good about myself and shake off the defeat.
You always thought the grass was greener, on the other side
Now it's my chance to live a bit, no more need to hide.
My heart is full of love and I will patiently wait,
To give it to someone special, I'll leave that all to fate.
So be happy in your chosen path, as I will surely be,
You really did me a favour, when you set me free.

*Susan Abdulrahman*


## TEMPUS FUGIT

I look in the mirror and what do I see?
This person, a stranger, who stares back at me.
The silky smooth skin is now ravaged with time,
A reflection resembling nothing of mine.

Musician's fingers, tapered and long,
But who took my fingers? Something's gone wrong.
When did it happen, this 'old woman' stage?
Gnarled joints and fingers all twisted with age.

Biggest of eyes, as blue as the sea,
Now fading with time like the rest of me.
Where are my eyes, who stole my dream?
So hard to remember, what did it all mean?

Who took my youth, when did it go?
What was I doing, why didn't I know?
Occupied being a mum and a wife,
I must have been busy, with something called *life*.

**Sue Desney-Hudson**

## THOSE WERE THE DAYS, SON

My hands were busy through the day,
I did not have much time to play.
I'd wash your clothes, I'd sew and cook,
But when you brought your picture book,
And ask me, please, to share your fun
I'd say, 'A little later, Son.'
I'd tuck you in all safe at night,
Hear your prayers, turn out the light.
Life is short, the years rush past,
A little boy grows up so fast.
No longer is he at your side,
His precious secrets to confide -
The picture books are put away,
There are no longer games to play.
No goodnight kiss, no prayers to hear,
That all belongs to yesteryear.

**S Rouse**

## PAPER CHASE

Smell the darkness.
Suddenly real, almost tangible,
A wake-up call in my mind,
Like the quick flare of a match.
The love buried under oceans, what lies beneath?

Familiar pieces begin to surface and join,
Form together to make a jigsaw.
A dream-like image floats before me,
But as I grasp at it,
It smudges itself out.

The pearly clouds, ones that hover over
Princesses' castles, now vanish
Far in the distance.
Ghosts fly from my frantic hands.
I can only read and remember - a mere fairytale.

The fear of forgetting what was once familiar.
What was once familiar, now fades.
The last pieces of that jigsaw lost, not found.
The care she took painting her lips, the smooth touch of her hand,
The only pieces I have.

The smell pierces the air as it pierces my heart.
Her perfume, the subtle hint of flowers, unseen.
I want to remember but the flame slowly dies.
Whatever I try to draw, rubs itself out.
Invaded by darkness; why does my drawing lack colour?

I cannot seem to pierce through the wrapping to that vibrant world.
Lonely. Trapped. Boxed in my own old age.
All that is collected is dead petals, covered by layers of dust.
Forever lost in a maze,
Never finding the right path.

*Kathryn West*

## SECRET SHAME

I'll tell you a story, which will seem rather sad,
Of a young Irish girl, whose life was drudgery and hell.
A God fearing Catholic who knew right from wrong.
She dreamed of attending the local dance,
Went against her parents' wishes.
The forbidden fruit at first is sweet,
But the price to be paid has a lasting bitterness beyond the grave.
Her dream reality, a nightmare ensued,
Frightened and lonely, a young girl raped.
Confession to God, no option,
She silently carried the child within.
One day an almighty row erupted.
Hatred for her attacker, contempt for her life of slavery,
The truth like venom she spat.
In blind shameful rage
The child was beaten from her belly.
Disowned and homeless, she fled her homeland.
Alone and bewildered, a stranger on a distant shore.
Secret foundations supported 40 years.
A life of mixed blessings, mostly good,
Those bad accepted as punishment due.
Never a word passed her lips,
Of the endurance she suffered.
Tested by God, she redeemed herself,
Finding strength and compassion to love seven children,
As though they were the blood that pumped through her veins,
So judge not on revelations
Accept that the foundations for the future,
Are built on the mistakes of the past.
Build with confidence, memories to hold dear to the heart.

*Annette Murphy*

## SUFFOLK

Something lingers in the evening,
Sits by the fire at supper,
Haunts the house in the night,
Interrupts my dreams in the dawn.
It pulls me from my slumber,
It will sing to me for all eternity,
No mind to conjure the melody.
I resist,
But it bursts into my head,
Thrusts me outside.
I am driven down a lane,
Still not fully conscious of the world,
The world not conscious of me.
I stumble up the hill,
Close my eyes as I reach the summit.
Sit on the soft earth,
And manipulate my mind,
Then my lids part slowly,
And my gaze meets the land beyond.
The rainbow ends here.
Ahead is the pot of gold,
Where the colours blend back into landscape.
The vibrant purples scream to me from the soil,
The astounding yellow fields of oil seed rape
Beckon to me from where I stand.
I go to them,
Flying through villages,
Glancing at single, insignificant buildings,
Dodging as the years come flying back,
Leaving a little something scattered somewhere,
Just to make sure they'll not be forgotten.

The bells chime four times as I pass,
The perpendicular church touching the sky.
I look out on the world Gainsborough and Constable
Looked upon so many years ago.

*Samantha Pryke (12)*

# FIRST LIGHT

It was July 30$^{th}$, year 1922
When I first came into view
How fast the time has sped away,
Seeming to go quicker, day by day.

So many things happening in that era,
Another great war, getting nearer.
I wonder if mankind will *ever* learn
That it's peace on Earth, for what we yearn?

That black day came, shattering dreams!
The world's gone mad, or so it seems.
The whole world seemed to be at war
Is that what mankind is destined for?

So much grief, and so much strife,
With such a terrible waste of life.
Maybe with sense, there will be one day
Hope that peace may come to stay.

Let love and care rule every heart,
To me that seems the best way to start.
All it needs is for the world to give
Absolute peace so *all* may live.

*Eddie Lawrence*

## BARBARA

Twelve years ago come October, to Cambridge I came merrily,
The widower of a relation, had asked if he might marry me,
In Oakington village his home was, green countryside all around,
One shop, not many houses, vast difference from my busy town.
Each day was a trip of discovery, see things I had not seen before,
Neighbours were so warm and friendly, each time I went out of
                                                                                  my door.
We lived in a small council bungalow, he music taught,
                                                  making cash spin.
I learned to run an allotment, then all my produce froze in.
For eight years we blissfully shared life, then fate cut into desire.
After long weeks in hospital, he left to sing in heavenly choir.
Four years alone I've kept busy, even was flooded this year,
But my good friendly neighbours, were there when I wanted them near.
To town I don't want to go back, my heart is in Cambridgeshire now,
Each year as I'm getting older, I want to stay here where they plough.
So many things I have seen here, the people chat to on each morn,
Dressed in their warm country clothing, stitched carefully if it is torn.
Most will address me as Barbara, expect their first name in return,
They treat you straight and you must do, same, is the first
                                                          thing you learn.
There's no second chances for cheaters, it simply is not
                                                      worth your while,
They look up and greatly respect you, if you live life in good style.
I walk up the road head held proudly, people I meet wish me well,
I've earned my place in this village, will stay till the Lord rings His bell.
Then I will sleep as the just do, in the long rest of mankind
Knowing I have done my best to be as the star I'll now shine.

*Barbara Goode*

## ONE MORE TIME
*(Dedicated to Arthur Charles Pacey
1915 - 1996)*

When you love someone
Never say goodbye.
Always say I love you,
Because you never know
If that's the last time
You'll ever gaze on their face again.

That night when I left you
Ill in your hospital bed,
Family moving noisily around us,
I looked into your grey, sad eyes and said
'Goodbye.'

Why that night of all nights, didn't I tell you
As I always did before I left
I love you?
Did we know as I kissed and left you
That it would be the last time?

Why did you go?
You left before I said
All the things I meant to say
But never said.
Deep feelings stored in my heart,
I hope you knew my heart.

Will I get the chance to tell you?
Is death the end
Or just a new beginning?
When my time comes
Will I get one more time to say
I love you Dad?

**Susan Watson**

## A Cantabrigian Abroad

I would love to be in Cambridge when the year is at the spring,
As the snowdrops first and the aconites show winter is on the wing.
The 'backs' in all their glory, the river's sluggish flow -
But, I am in a far off land and I cannot homeward go!
Here, the sun shines day by day, the sky stays sapphire blue.
There the rain is gentle, the storms are short and few.
They slip from spring to summer, they glide from day to night.
Here, everything is too intense and every day too bright.
The grass is green in Cambridge, here, it's orange, yellow, brown.
No dust storms blow in Cambridge, my gentler, greyer town.
History towers over all in this 'cradle of mankind',
I prefer the home-made version that's so tender on my mind.

I long to see a primrose, buttercups and cowslips fair.
Let me go home to Cambridge, because my heart's still there!

*J M Jones*


## Spring 1985

Spring blossom
Gently frothing,
Wind roaring,
Tearing, tossing,
Rain splashing,
Hail slashing.
Can this really be spring?
Yes, here's the sun
Touching every lovely thing
And a rainbow bringing joy
That only a rainbow can bring.

**Edith Tyrrell**

## MY PRAYER

In the morning, when dewdrops fall from the spider's web
I think of you.
In the afternoon's sunshine,
I think of you
And in the evening song,
I hear you.
When the skies draw dark and the stars sparkle,
I see you.
I see you, my Creator in everything abound,
The beauty of the day, the stillness of the night
I feel your Holy Spirit guiding me in all that I do.
In all that's good and beautiful, there also is the bad,
So Lord, when I thank you for all that I have,
Remind me of those who have nothing.
           Amen

*Jenny Johnson*


## A VERY SPECIAL OCCASION

Little Sammy will never forget the day,
When the tractor rally came this way.
Such a good friendly atmosphere
As neighbours sat out to clap and cheer.
Out came cups of tea and glasses of wine,
What a blessing that the weather was fine.
Sammy sat on Daddy's lap, impressed by it all,
As tractors went by, very large and small.
Pulling farm carts on which families sat waving,
Decorated with flags, balloons and bunting.
How fortunate this happened to be a chosen location,
Thus turning into a very special occasion.

*I L Wright*

## Crossing Fen Country

the sky is higher than a giant's hurl
an unseen starlet skylark uncurls its skein of song
the earth is as dark and rich as mediaeval images of hell
the lines are straight - furrows, roads, rails and channels

the flat fecundity of lurking, marsh-clad fen
is laid bare, like artists' anatomical studies
of flesh disrobed of skin:
are these features fit to be seen?

In this subcutaneous world, water flows uphill
drain and dike gather the oozed lymph and lift it
cautiously into leam and lode and on until
it reaches man-moved rivers built to save, not spill

cuts are raised up like chalices above the congregational marl
my thoughts meander by the infidelity of water levels' fickle fluids
this may have been mountain range, plain, primeval plankton-chowder,
                                                           or gentle hill
the chance of change makes my blood-pump pump harder before
                                                           it's still

*David Xeno*


## Jesus Green

When the sky is clear, paradise is reflected
in this pool. Brightness seems assured
in the mural lambency, the moment mid
air from the impossible diving board

when weightless, the athlete considers gravity
and like all ponderous treasures takes a while to sink.
Smooth-haired boys wait to flip up booty;
one, shock-headed white, stops where the wing

stirred water slows limbs in butterfly.
Events, precluded by the strolling lifeguards
watching Grace stretch to five lengths a day,
stop at unblown whistles and their games of cards.

*Hannah Langworth*


## CELTIC MAN

She carries his smile with her,
Pockets it, treasures it, studies it,
Mostly covers it, blankets it
Muffles the razor sharp pain,
Of that sudden wide smile of the lean Irishman
Who walked through her mind
With a looseness of limb and a long, easy stride.
He with the high, chiselled cheek bones,
The pain lines and furrows
Etched in tough leathered skin,
Tenderness stretched over years.

She is haunted in daylight and dreams
By the ghost of the stooped, sloe-eyed man
With the magical songs of the Celts in his blood,
He with the sun and the light in his hair,
The past in his eyes and the rhymes in his heart,
He with the long, brown hands
That wove pictures and words in the air,
The bones and the fingers splayed wide,
Gently touching and probing and tracing the lines
And the veins of the pain that he placed
Like a stone at the base of her heart.

*Carmel Wright*

## An Honest Luck

A gentle man walks on with bag alone;
Draws heavy on his pipe with merry face.
He turns his back on memories old to find anew,
The wonders of a life with fields of gold.

A flurry of fair geese do fly ahead
From dunes of sand and Nile's enriched with jewels,
And banquish in delights of season's sun,
All merry with their finds of polished stone.

A tree doth stand in solitude, awatch,
Of workers buried deep in autumn's show,
And tedious gatherings of parched, unruly crops.
Many people bend with fingers hard,
Who's nimble ends do tear at summer's seed once sewn.

A creature of the blackened, dampened earth,
Reveals its naked eye unto the land.
It travels far to find a water's flow.
Alas, so many thirsty crops have drunk their fill.

The man will find his end watched by this tree,
Breathing deep the pipe whipped by those winds.
The mole will look upon his charred remains
And smile as smoke still rises from thy dusty end.
These geese will eat the fields with broken wings
Now torn by ruthless winds; make ill thy soul.

The tree will take remaining riches of these lands,
And in pursuit of bountiful attire,
Displays the fruits from all its entity,
And promise nought to all those furrowed brows.

All from this shall look on with dismay
And flounder in thy winter's true ablaze.
Now black with ebony, lament thy soul,
Once full with life and flight, now drained into the soil.

If ever 't were a man in glee, despite,
His loss of golding fields and loss of pipe,
Then touch my cheek, and heart, displayed but once.
He sits upon an ever rising cloud,
So high that no hand may ever touch,
Unless they seek true light or wonderment.
He watches over faint and weary souls,
Who some may lack a faith in this tall tale;
And so, upon his brow which never shyed,
A feast of stones now black from burning fire;
They sit in all his glory and delight,
The once lost jewels and riches of the Nile.

*Tiffany Tondut*


# THORPE MEADOWS
*(In early autumn)*

Aged tangled branches of crab apple and pear,
Rowan trees and elderberry, drip with loads of fruit.
Higher and yet higher, stretch tall poplars in straight rows
Reaching to the heavens, with wreaths of mist between.

Alternately, autumnal sunshine breaks through with streaks of light
Forming its lines of dappled shade beneath the foliated ground,
Whilst insects and small mammals dart and scurry through damp leaves
Along the dew-filled grass and hedge which margin waterside.

Watch the reflections cast their patterns on the river Nene,
Graceful swans gliding by necks high, and ducks with broods between,
All breathes security and peace,
Deep love enfolds this scene.

*A R Cubitt*

## POVERTY AT ITS BEST

Jamaica's warmth at its best,
Stands out on its own, from the rest,
Poverty and sunshine, a wonderful place,
Friendly people, with no rat race.

Sipping a Red Stripe beer is the thing to do,
Or sample cocktails, and a big bamboo.
So many bananas grow in one bunch,
And coconuts every where, waiting to munch.

32 varieties of Appleton rum
Shouldn't try them all, you'll have a bad tum,
Only the Over-Proof, it's got to be best
You'll love it so much, you'll forget the rest.

In Ocho Rio's you'll find bargains galore
Haggle in the market, elsewhere you'll pay more,
And rafts made for two, a bit of romance,
Or there's Reggae music, if you feel like a dance.

Kingston Town's Bob Marley land
Rastaman folk, remember his band?
And stately Deven House, the country's pride
Had lunch in the grounds, couldn't eat inside.

The amazing Y S Falls, is such a pretty trip
Where you can stop, cool off, or take a dip.
Or a Catamaran cruise, with plenty of booze
Party spirit of course, then take a snooze.

And Dunn's River Falls, climb to the top
But you need special shoes, it's such a big drop
Try a Black River cruise, a crocodile swamp
Trees with egrets that fall, and vanish in a champ.

Blue Mountain coffee, the world's best,
We sampled a cup when we paused to rest,
Old shacks built on edges of a cliff face
And women washing in streams, is no disgrace.

Seven miles of Negril's beach of white sand,
And Montego Bay, for the rich and grand.
There's colourful fish on the sea bed
But watch the sunset, when the sea turns red.

Simple but happy, Jamaicans live,
Relaxed and carefree, always willing to give.
Pure white teeth, and such a big smile
Possessions mean nothing, when you think awhile.

*Mary McNulty*


## MISTAKE IN AFGHANISTAN

50 were killed in a village today -
An Afghan village; it was a mistake,
Should have been other Afghans they said -
Innocent villagers, homes and kids,
Not in an office high up in New York,
But dead in the dusty mountains
In mud huts on the edge of existence -
Only 50, and just a mistake -
Couldn't be seen by the B52s -
Died in the houses with their children,
Whole families probably, living their lives
On the edge of the world where they shouldn't have been;
For we comfortable folk have decided
That they should be saved from . . .
From what? When the land is so poor,
And they are half-starved?
Perhaps they are better off dead.
Now *there's* a comforting thought!

*Stephen Morse*

## YOUR FINAL HOURS

Oh Chris, your time is nearly here,
You've grown so thin and weak it's clear.
I've watched you struggle these last few days,
You've gone downhill in so many ways.
Today it's Monday and your wheelchair we'll get,
To take you about, so you'd better get set.
We can go to the shops and all over the place,
We must put a smile back on your face.
It's Tuesday now and to football we'll go,
They won 3-0, well don't you just know.
It's the first they've won for many a game,
You were happy and smiled, you were glad you came.
When all was over, it was home and to bed,
You'd had a good time but were tired you said.
At half-past twelve you took a turn for the worst,
The pain was so bad, you started to curse.
We called out the doctor who came very quick,
Oh Chris, she could do nothing, you were so sick.
Your breathing was laboured, you were clammy but cold,
I lay by your side, your hands to hold.
Just before two you called the boys to come,
We were all holding hands but feeling so numb.
'I love you all' was the last words you spoke,
Then went into a coma from which you never awoke.
I laid by your side feeling utter despair,
Why must God take you, it isn't fair.
At half-past four with one last gasp you died
The boys and I, we cried and cried.
You'd lived life to the full even tho' you were ill,
But thro' pain and discomfort you had the will.

Your funeral took place, so many people came,
Nearly four hundred, many I couldn't name.
You were so well thought of in all that you did,
You'll live on forever, well done kid!
I loved you so dearly, I'll never forget you,
Wherever I am or whatever I do.
You were my life for twenty odd years,
I have plenty of memories and also tears.
Rest in peace my darling, I'll be with you one day.
      My love forever
                  Shirley

***Shirley Fordham***


## TRANSACTION

Tears drop
From a scared pair of eyes,
The transaction begins
From the Earth to the skies
Vision becomes cryptic.
The soul cries
Suddenly
Everything's beautiful, like the sun's rise.

Years of hurt
And tears of pain.
Maybe this is for the best,
Let me explain,
Finally I'm at rest,
Separated from humanity,
Everything silent and dark,
Sorry, beloved family.

***David Hall***

## SIGHT, SOUND AND SENSATION

Pleasant is the twilight hour that stays
Twixt evening and the night,
When the slanting sun sends its last rays
To touch the trees with gilded light.

The scented blooms in bold relief,
Colours in contrast with the shade,
As though painted with artistic brief,
Before the magic moment fades.

Music is for some the catalyst,
That sends the soul up to the skies,
And all frustrations then untwist,
Sets the spirit free in paradise.

Yet more glorious is the morning hour,
When from fretful sleep to rise
And stand beneath the crystal shower,
Such cleansing power to realise.

Cascading water, hot then cold,
Saturation's steaming glove,
Sheets of water that unfold,
Baptismal blessing from above.

Whatsoever, then your delight may be,
Scent or sound or visual hour,
That which greatest pleasures me,
Is a blissful soaking 'neath my shower.

*Richard Styles*

# GREAT ST MARY'S CAMBRIDGE

Within the city bounds
Her bells they sing
In empty streets
On a lazy Sunday morn

Barefoot on rounded cobbles
I tiptoe across the market square
And guildhall clock strikes 11

Café on pavement
Shielded by large umbrella
Just opening its doors
Ready for queuing tourists
The smell of garlic bread
Already pungent in the air

Great St Mary's surveys the view
As already people climb her tower
Armed with camera
And plenty of puff

Market traders
They know me now
Ignore my presence
Bare foot
On my way to write
Another poem.

*Moira Clelland*

## Invading Our Territory

The male tit
displayed
in front of the patio windows
daring me to come out,
hovering on wings
beating
innumerable times a second.

A pair of great tits
had made their nest
in the hollow base
of our ornate patio wall,
swooping in and out
of the tiny space between
the layers of stone supports.

Hopping among the branches
of the purple lilac tree
overhanging the wall,
they chittered their defiance,
darting to the nest-site
when the coast was clear
of cats and humans
and predatory magpies.

In the house
we watched
like anxious parents
willing their survival,
guarding their privacy,
chasing off unwanted visitors,
longing for the first glimpse
of the fledglings
and ensuring their flight to freedom.

But suddenly
busyness ceases,
the birds have flown.
The nest is empty
cleaned and tidied
for another year.
We miss them.

*Beryl Johnson*

## AN ANGEL AT DAWN

An angel floated down from Heaven
And landed on the lawn,
Floated down from Heaven
To greet the brand new dawn.

The angel had a radiance
That glowed amidst the dew,
A radiance never seen before,
With colours that were new.

Aqua-pink and ultra-marine,
Golden - navy too;
With shimmering light, translucence bright,
And many shades of blue.

Colours reflected in the sky
Of new day dawning bright,
With swirling shades of light and dark
To chase away the night.

The angel stood upon the lawn
With eyes raised to the sky,
With wings unfurled, and arms spread out,
To teach the world to fly.

*Valerie Ann Knight*

## KNOCK AND IT SHALL BE OPENED UNTO YOU

Faith is a gift from God
Give me this gift I pray,
Or under a graveyard sod
Shall I unknowing lay?

Others have received I know
The gift only He bestows.
Their happy faces tell me so
Shining with an inward glow.

So long, too long have I searched
And 'many knots unravelled'.
Still I stumbled as I lurched
And 'in and out' I travelled.

The only way I see plain
Is to follow where He guides,
Then perchance He will deign
The door to open wide.

Yet stay! I only have to knock,
That is what He surely said,
His door has never had a lock,
So what have I to dread?

Oh Saviour open up to me,
Give me purpose for my life,
At last, long last, I shall see
An ending to my strife.

The gift is mine at long last!
The cross I bore now light,
Doubts and fears are now past,
Heavenly visions in my sight.

Challenges presented every day
Give opportunities to prove,
If you ask for help each time you pray
The mountains will surely move.

With this armour face the world,
You will find you can repel
Satan's banner remains unfurled,
His hordes you will dispel.

Fight the good fight with all Thy might,
Win the prize beyond all gold.
His face keep within Thy sight
And join the heavenly fold.

*Pamela Willison*


## THE 1886 CAROUSEL

Taking pride of place in the Fairground by the sea
The 1886 gallopers call out to me.
Organ music cascades down over the little Victorian seaside town
Reflections of colour, a majestic jewel in the crown.

Suspended in past times, if only for a second it seems
A chance to re-live your childhood dreams.
The starting bell rings out, time to hold on tight
Rustic tones of elegant fowl in flight.

Gentle mares with manes and tails that float on the summer breeze,
Signs asking ladies to ride side-saddle please.
Even the grandparents and aunties pay
To ride behind in a rich golden sleigh.

Handsome black stallions with nostrils aflair
A challenging ride, if you dare,
The thundering of hooves echo out to sea
Then come racing back to me.
Nostalgic past times to the present day,
The enchantment of the carousel is just a gallop away

*Louise King*

## CASTOR HANGLANDS

Uninvited to those still and ancient Hanglands
From Roman days or beacons from a Celtic clan
The hill of trees, past forest from another time
Of charcoal burners or keepers of the Consul's vine.

No welcome here, as brambles thick with thorn
Emerge like guards, through brackens tangled form
Tearing the unwary, restraining, bar the way
As wire-whipping barbs, grow strong throughout the clay.

Earth's retreating frosts, gouge sleek the treacle ground
Ferns crumble under footholds, each frond a powdered brown
This heavy strides an effort, it's hostile and unkind
These woods can do without us and forces us to mind.

It seems to have no yielding, yet, just beyond our gaze
A flock of sheep, wool matted, huddle quiet to graze
Heads turn to stare, black faced, with large enquiring eyes
This peaceful scene beguiles us, beneath the evening skies.

Tall pines protect this landscape as evidence appears
When cloven hoof and barking, betrays the shy roe deer
Close-by the sacred holly, attesting Saturn's night
Tho' berries, red since autumn, proclaim a godly light.

*Pat Homer-Wooff*

## PASSING

As days go by and night turns to light,
Every day is new and oh so bright.
Attaining new goals and reaching a new personal height.
Doing tasks no time to bask as time is so tight.
Caring, sharing and doing things that seem so right.
Very soon light turns back to night.

*Andrew Crump*

## Turn To The Lord

If you feel forsaken
And your sin's too great
To be forgiven.
Take your troubles to the Lord
Yes, if you want rid of them.
For He knows your every weakness,
Your quality of thought.
And He'll never fret
If you use Him
As your last resort.

So open up your heart today
To the king of kings.
Sample plenty of His mercy
Then hear the voice of purity sing.
'For He is the fountain
Of expectation and true love
And your spotless soul
Craves only for the Lord above.'

*David Ashley Reddish*


## Stepping Stone

How young and dear you looked,
although worried about your job,
and marriage around the corner.
Desiring to be hooked -
and me chief mourner -
for the days gone by
but on your wedding day,
I promise not to cry.

*Pearl Cornwell*

## THE BRICK YARD

When we used to walk our dogs
In morning sun and evening fogs
At the brick yard

We saw graffiti on the wall
With words so strong you could hear them call
At the brick yard

Rude words are written in green ink
Well, do you know what I think?
You . . .
Stick a person in the heart
With turquoise eyes that fire steel darts

You looked as if you'd just been slapped
When you saw that green in at
The brick yard
Green words screamed with angry strife
'Kevin needs to get a life!'
At the brick yard
Are you shir - your heart can't - ley
Have you asked your feelings why?

Pat
A cake
Pat
A cake
The writing's on the wall
You're not so greasy after all
I miss our walks, I miss our talks
I miss your joke about candles and forks
At the brick yard

I miss your funny little song
As we used to walk along
At the brick yard

And though my love for you can't die
I guess it's time to say goodbye
To the brick yard

**Margaret Cryer**


## FRIENDS

A friend will understand, be there for you
whenever you feel sad,
When things go wrong they'll cheer you up
then you won't feel so bad.
Real friends won't take offence
When angry words are said,
Will still be waiting for your call,
Ready to forgive though you may cause them pain
You'll soon be laughing once again.
And friends that stay together
Through all the growing years,
Who shared the bad times
Who shared the troubles and the fears,
Are always there to give a helping hand
Who know you well and always understand.
True friends will hold you close
If sorrow comes your way.
Will listen, will comfort you each day
Throughout your life whatever fate may send,
You know there's always someone there.
A special person,
*Your best friend.*

**Margaret Pay**

## The Gift Of Life

When I woke up this morning
I saw a light shining from up high
The clouds drifting along in a gentle breeze
Now and again, the rustle of the leaves
The dew glistens on the grass left by the cool night air.
The spiders have been busy
Spinning their webs, they cling to every bow.
Like lace sewn with pearls they are everywhere,
A dewdrop in the eye of every rose, sparkles like a tear.
The scent of the earth, fresh from a shower,
The air so sweet it overpowers.
I just want to linger there for hours
As I open wide my window
It brings a tear and a sigh for
Why should God want me to share
So much peace and beauty on all sides.
I give thanks for the chance I have had
To walk this ground
For the richness of the gift of life is the greatest to be found.

*Joan Wright*


## Prayer For Here And Now

Move me, this early week of spring, to hear
Birdsong that interrupts my sleeping heart.
Lift me, while winds and rain of March blow wet,
To watch the flattened grasses rise and part.

Catch me lest falling tempts my doubting soul,
Stand me up straight and make me know I'm strong.
Guard me and guide me while my timeless self
Puts past and future in their time-worn song.

Hold me before I bow my head below
The wringing weather in the trying gale.
Help me to kiss the moment's flying grace
And give the lie to time's beguiling tale.

*John Brackenbury*


## UNTITLED

The money machine tells me that it is indisposed
And not inclined to give me £20
Even though I know my pin number
Even though it's Sunday
It says that it is sorry
And asks if I have some other request
Such as
Knowing my bank balance
Or would I like to order a new bank manager
This Sunday is a grey so pewter
And so water retentive
That I lean my arm on the wall
And speak to the lime green glow
I would like to request something please
A freshly cooked Tobermory lobster
With a tossed salad
Served on Lalique
And accompanied by two bottles of
Tattinger 1985 on a tray inlaid
With Quetzal feathers, frosted
Oh and a small goats cheese from
The Languedoc, thank you
My card sticks back out at me
like a tongue.

*Marina Yedigaroff*

## BLACK HEARTED

Window of trauma throughout life opens,
Innermost secrets cut up and bleeding.
Shaking uncontrollably feeling kicked about,
A spell turns without a word.
Morning breakthrough gently concerns.
Rock bottom crying, broken.
Unearthed so deeply within, memory search.
Facing a misguided episode breathing inside,
Regardless of this life, tragedy hanging.
Complicated sources buried, old haunts returned,
Darkness from my heart disappears.
Cooling down emotion, without fighting, invades,
Nervous attitudes from everyday facilities.
Fulfilling everybody is somewhere, transofrmation's vital,
Calculated fixed story, knowing where you're going,
Day after day, passing by, grass growing under your feet.
Worst last thought claimed imprisonment of life,
Unforgettable obligation came back, sentenced beyond.
Hidden carnage constantly demoralised.
Evil infected development, cursed influences,
Frustration melted from stillness, puzzled waking.
Reaching clear ground, standing - empty.
Alternative revealed associate, disturbing dilemma,
Jealous situation personal problem, over and over,
Forced compromise revealed unbearable surroundings.
Location kept us guessing, endure familiar comeback.
Realistic intelligence at war, personal stench,
Experience signifies escaped detection.
Fuming relentless taste welcome, spooky silence,
Declaring possibilities determined success.
Recent sound mending, departure pleasant.
Traumatic rift caused past behaviour.
Rebounds repeatedly shamed intention, planning dreaming.
Endless performance affectionately barricaded, 24/7.
Discovering time alone becomes refreshing,

Falling asleep, events are over.
Remorseful letters described serious allegations.
Secured, concerned, without hope, restore seal,
Overnight chances claimed rapturous win.
Possible luck beyond emotional pleasant dreams.
Selective high standards, portray personalities.
Abundantly breaking from principle cause.
Wasting ambitions just made a sandstorm.
Rocks and stones, no one hears.
Figure carrying a bundle of faded news.

*Sharron Hollingsworth*


## THE QUEEN'S JUBILEE

The Queen's Jubilee, 50 wonderful years,
She lost her sister and mother, there were quite a few tears,
But a resilient lady is our Queen,
In our lifetime, the best we have seen.

During the Jubilee, she has travelled to many places,
She was met by hundreds of happy smiling faces.
Our Queen to this country has been loyal and true,
Through many troubled times she has always come through.

Republicans are plotting to dethrone our Monarchy,
They don't realise this will create anarchy,
They want a President to rule this land,
But we Royalists are determined to keep this happy band.

They want a Republic what ever the cost,
Otherwise the Queen's pomp and pageantry will be lost.
But we Royalists are true and will have no fears,
Because our Monarchy will last for many, many years.

*Robert Baslington*

## The Dark And Half Past

As far away as next door
And as close as the neighbours
Last year this time, next, you, I
Wonder out, what do I want? What
Don't I? Why not? Holding on out
Brightly hands drowsy together
This far so quiet, faith without
Or inside belief precisely, some
Comfort, comfortable doubt, and
Doubtful pride in shades of one
And another, scratching to vague
In a sober drink-dazed arrogance
And resignation acting for real
Both as if it were obvious
Choice with no free-will, and
Whether it matters or acting
Or not, whether we think we
See everything, in from what we mean,
Or if we think we see what we feel
When it's only what there is to see,
Still you are the most, the only,
Beautiful I've ever been or will.

*Antony Picking*


## My Shadow

Oh there you are again,
You are always following me,
Every time I look behind me you are there,
See I walk across the garden and you come too,
Okay if you are not going to go away
I think we can be friends.

*Charlotte Gibbons  (10)*

# I Saw You

I saw you.
In the unfurrowed faces of the young.
Untouched by blood red,
Not clogged by brown mud,
Or marred by grey stinking, stagnant pools.
I saw you.
In life-drained white marble.
The killing conformity of regimented rows.
Hidden beneath carefully trimmed grass,
The green blanket fails to obliterate
Craters and trenches.
Edges softened over time
Rain falls, wind blows
But you lay still,
The harsh finality.

*Nicola Grant*


# Cleatham, Lincolnshire

Pitted, yellowed bones reveal themselves.
Windswept hillside, place of rest.
A framework only, to hang the soul on.
A familiar assemblage in eternal sleep.

It isn't she who was,
But still our minds attempt
To clothe with flesh, status and possessions,
An Anglo-Saxon woman.

Were she but here to know our calm deductions,
Why she is thus not ash as others are.
Why silver beads adorn her neck,
Among black urns with slabs depressing.

*Dianne Roberts*

## JIM

There're good things and there're bad things
That always is the way,
But you, my special someone
Keep the bad at bay.

Whenever I am lonely
In complete silent solitude . . .
When it's about to turn ugly
You show up and change my mood.

When I get paranoid,
Become jealous and green
The right words come out of your mouth
And everything turns brighter than it once seemed.

When darkness has me in its grip
When I feel there's no hope left,
You calm me down and hold me
In your arms I can safely rest.

*Jodie McKane*


## CAMBRIDGE ON THE MOVE

This city of two - the time-honoured gown
enclosing the center - an updated town.
Tradition or progress? It's nothing but trouble
in this ancient city whose role is now double.
We can only come in on our bikes, or the buses
and rarely we mix - the 'thems' and the 'usses'.

But however you go, when all's done and said
I'll go it alone, and travel 'a pied'!

*Helen Walker*

## ODE TO A BROTHER

Reuben Law's the best brother a man can have,
He's the man you can depend on through nature's pitfalls.
You can depend on him, through life's crises and bearing
　　　　　　　　　　　　　　　　　　　　other's crosses.
Regardless of life and limb, whether it be kith or kin.
Familiar faces through grandchildren grow.
If you must reap, you must first sow.
To daughter's delight through teens and 20s of father's wish that
　　　　　　　　　　　　　　　　　　　　there be plenty.
Absentees of wish we could
Oh brother, your 80$^{th}$ birthday should be of the happiest wishes
Through millennium century.

***Raymond Law***


## LAMP-MAID JANE'S POEM
## FRUIT YIELDS AROUND NENE RIVER

Anne Coleman enjoys nice red fruit in July,
Ripe plums now so big, some fruits too hath fallen,

Even into Nene River flowing freely,
Pebbles below, on the riverbed sliding,

Pushed with the current, become molten jewels,
Reeds, rape and radishes grow in the lowlands.

Mice make their nests in cornfields and in coalbarns,
A coalman also keeps pigs, in the Fenlands.

Under a roof of iron, piglets squeal lively,
Then sadly empty, as they go marketing.

***Louis Don Barrow***

## THE GREAT FLOODS

The crows are building high this year
They seem to know the floods are near.
Badgers move to higher ground
Even the ducks are leaving town.
Fox's den is free to view,
He's long since joined the queue
To find a home on drier ground
So that his children shall not drown.
But, oh the folly of modern man
Nowhere to go.
He builds on ground that's far too low,
He builds on marshland and old ponds
His ancestors once had fished upon.
He's filled in dykes where years ago
All flood water used to flow.
In mid-summer these marshlands seem
The perfect place to build your dreams.
Rivers Ouse, Derwent, Trent and Don,
They're banks should not be built upon,
For in wet winters to man's cost,
His home, his possessions, may be awash.
So, remember when you're looking for a home
Hunt round to find you're not alone,
For the instinct of some animals may just guarantee,
That you, your home and family,
Won't end up washed out to sea.

*W Oliver*

## THE WORLD IS WONDERFUL

The heather's blooming
on the Dunes.
The birds all sing
their merry tunes.

The sun is shining.
the world is gay.
What a wonderful
mid-summer day.

*Julie Brown*


# FAITH

I know that you are with me Lord
in your omnipresent way
I know you hear me sigh
and listen to all I say.

Help me reflect
and never reject
problems may be insurmountable
your love,
my faith, helps them to melt away.

I know that you are with me Lord
as I kneel to pray
clasping my more mortal hands
respectful to bow my head
I rejoice
in your ways I am led.

Better things
Positive schemes
Hopes and dreams
I pray

and know,
that you are with me Lord.

*Valerie Hewson*

## THE DAISY
*(Dedicated to Tal)*

You frolic through the grass;
Unheeding of the fast approaching doom.
Your resurrection waiting in a tranquil pause.
Your re-creation time span reassures.

As measured footsteps, guiding rolling blades,
Straight lines with merciless precision
Delight the trousered reaper's overpass.
Your bowing head in transitory submission.

As evening hush with birdsong correlates.
And man reflects with pride upon his day.
New life, untouched by human hands transmits
New birth, new growth. New flowering underlays.

**Mary E Calthrop**


## LLEWELLYN

Llewellyn has come in out of the dark
His fingers spread like winter nights
His garments worn as ragged leaves.
Straddled over the sand
Spread-eagled over the sleeping dunes
Living his life in his ancestors,
Sleeping his time in pockets of gold
Saving himself for the time of New Beginnings.
His bones are iron and his tongue is still,
He has no face and every face.
In the time of the sleeping skulls
Llewellyn lies.
In the time of the Great Warriors
Llewellyn is Chief.

***Patricia Crouter***

## THE UNIVERSE

What is beyond the azure blue sky
Where nearer to Earth snow-white cumulus fly?
We know there's the planets which we see when it's dark
And the luminous glow of the moon o'er the park
And then there's the millions of bright sparkling stars
Which twinkle near Jupiter, Venus and Mars.
When after a storm a rainbow appears from nowhere
Like magic its pastel bridge rears
Then slowly it vanishes, disappears from our view
Leaving no trace of its delicate hue.
During a storm come the flashes of light
And the roll of the thunder in the still of the night,
The diaphanous rain riding winds of gale force
Suddenly stops! Nature's back on her course.
An erupting volcano, a splitting earthquake
Heavy falls of deep snow may leave floods in their wake.
We are bound by the elements and can't get away
From events in our lives which we face day by day
But there's one thing we know in our hearts that is sure
That these powers almighty which fill us with awe
Are sent by the Lord who reigns up above
And watches the universe with heavenly love.
We don't know if there's life in the eternal sky
Far beyond view of mortal eye
We can travel in space from this world through the air
And to depths of the sea, marine life to compare
But the visions beyond are withheld from our sight
They belong to the Lord of all power and might.
One day when from this world we depart
We may see further beauty to gladden the heart
Till then we must strive to accept what life brings
Until our soul leaves us on heaven-bound wings.

*Enid Hewitt*

## DOWN MEMORY LANE

I remember winters long ago
When we had fun on ice and snow
Frost would last for weeks on end
Freezing ponds down in the Fens

I remember the blacksmith, years ago at work
Wearing a leather apron to protect his shirt
On the anvil he would beat red hot irons into shape
Shoeing horses for him was easy, like me, eating cake

I remember planes years ago, all had double wings
Flying above the treetop, missing everything
I remember that day at school when we dashed out of class
To see the German Zeppelin when over us it did pass

I remember the windmills of long ago
Four, five or eight sails round they would go
Grinding corn for the local bakery to make
Bread, buns and different kinds of cake

I remember when ha'pennies were two a penny
Spending a ha'penny at the sweet shop, if we had any
Many times we sat talking in the glow of firelight
In the dark paraffin lamps and candles we had at night

I know times have changed in so many ways
But for us our childhood days were happy days
We had fun and games and a laugh with others
And no exchange is possible, for the love of father and mother

*Harry Skinn*

## My Destiny

It could only be my destiny,
The odds were against us,
It happened so suddenly and I was free
And the cards didn't lie too, which was another plus.

You see there could never be another you
Or another me, because we both knew
We were worlds apart
And that was just the start.

How could two people meet
From different countries and another street?
This was never meant to be
If the heart doesn't feel, then the eyes don't see.

So how on Earth, could this be
She lived on the land and he on the sea,
When he sailed into her life at last,
It was destiny and everything happened so fast.

Time was their enemy, it went by too fast.
After setting eyes on each other, it could have been their last,
And now he had to sail away
That was a very sad day.

But as strange as it could be
That sad day was 50 years ago, you see
As we are still together today and will be until eternity
Because this was my destiny.

*Beryl Sylvia Rusmanis*

## FUN AND BLOOM

Oh what fun it is to be at Southend by the sea
lots of floss, ice cream and tea, and throwing pebbles out to sea
building castles on the sand and a moat that goes around

We have a pier a bit run down, fishermen like to try their ploy,
many suggestions have been put forth
the council just drag their feet some more.
As a kid I loved to collect shells on the beach
and paint all different colours and make into necklaces and
                                                fancy brooches.
The boats from the pier were magnificent,
The Daffodil, The Royal Sovereign,
They sailed to London Docks and back,
The Medway, such lovely memories.

Our parks are full of bloom, the gardeners work so hard
keeping them at their best, Priory Park is one of the best.
'Hands off our park,' we all say, given by R A Jones.

Just leave our green parks and belt alone,
We do not want a concrete jungle.
All these greedy cats with all their bundles
drive a road through their houses.
I'm sure this would please their spouses.

*Elsie Moore*


## WELCOME TO OUR HOME

Our home is humble - but be sure
A welcome greets you at the door,
A kindly hand extended out -
Sincerely offered there's no doubt.

We like the company of a friend,
A listening ear we have to lend,
A friendly word, some small advice,
*These* things we offer bear *no* price.

*E Jones (Betty)*

## BRIDGE OVER TROUBLED WATER

The bridge it towered into the sky
Supported by girders of steel
Beautifully made in every way
Its strength and power you feel
The mighty struts hold cables firm
Such precision in all its creation
It stands grandly for all to tread
Faith has no limitation
It provides a continuous route across
For Christians a way to go
Joining, connecting those in faith
Leaving behind the unwilling to know
Under the bridge in troubled waters
Is distress and worries and concern
People rushing back and forth
Who simply wouldn't learn
Illness, sadness, malfunction there
Deep waters running free
Spending money toned down and weak
People they couldn't see
The power over nature and the human race
As the bridge towers over the water
With its almighty strength and power
We grow in faith as bricks and mortar.

*Catherine Armstrong*

## Blackbirds Take To Wing

Suddenly, sable markings on the winter-white sky.
Hills like a ruffle round the sinking sun's ruddy face.
Shiver-cold comfort needing a warm cloak.
Dark fields hiding tomorrow's growth,
Appearing barren yet with a certain promise.
The soaring birds lift wings and hearts
Towards some distant couplings, some distant meetings.
The trees stand skeleton guard over their nooks and crannies
No longer clothed in leafy sheltering, but standing guard
Ready to receive new tenants at a later date.
The birds disappear, the shadowy grey replaces the white.
Wending our way home to warm fires and closed curtains.
We feel the year's aspirations fly away with the birds
Leaving us trudging in our earth-weighted boots.
And our hearts cannot sing as the blackbirds take to the wing.

*Polly Bennison*

## Untitled

We all know it will happen,
It's just a matter of where and when.
What will cause it we cannot know.
From the moment we are born, we embark upon a journey
towards our final destination.

But is it the end?
What lies beyond?
A void of nothingness, or new life?
We cannot explain nor really know the answer until the end,
when it makes no difference.

Family and friends are left behind,
Feeling angry and hurt, asking, 'Why?'
It all seems unjust and unfair.
Life's purpose is questioned, for if life should end why should it begin?

Each day our end draws closer,
Yet we still carry on living regardless
Without the uncertainties of what lies ahead being dwelt upon.
The only certainty is that where there is life there is death.

*Sophie Lianne Perkins*


## THANKS

Thanks for listening when I'm down!
Thanks for always being around.
You say you'll be there - then you're not!
Your excuse is - you forgot!
I need you sometimes when you're not there -
But I know you'll always care.
What am I gonna do when you're gone?
How am I ever gonna carry on?
Then who am I going to share my highs and lows
As along life's road we go?
I'd like to think you'll always be there -
But I know life isn't always fair.
I'd like to say - while I can,
'Thanks for listening,
Through my highs and lows,
As along life's road we go.
    Thanks.'

*Norma Spillett*

## New Experience

Don't ignore the music
Listen to the bells
Hear the choir singing
Believe in magic spells

Be steadfast at the cross-roads
Let none impede the way
Just once in every lifetime
The heart must have its say

Refuse the message if you dare
Avoid the easy track
With beating heart to guide you
There'll be no turning back

Plunge into the forest
Feel the briars sting
A heart that's found its haven
Can conquer anything

*Dennis Bensley*


## Doubt Not

Doubt that stars are clear and bright
On a cold December night.
Doubt that primroses bloom in the spring,
Wonder if skylarks know how to sing.
Doubt the beauty of roses in June,
'Ware the magic of a full clear moon.
Doubt that the oceans and skies are blue,
But never doubt that my love is true.

*A R Barnes*

## Dawn Awakening

The clock striking on the village green
The cockerel crowing
The whistling kettle
The cat . . . sitting

His pipe table
His golf bag
His fragrance . . . lingering
    Lavender smoke from the bonfire . . . drifting
The Virginia creeper
The nightingale
The ending of the day
The stairway clock . . .

    Awaiting the dawn!

***Carole King***

# SUBMISSIONS INVITED
*SOMETHING FOR EVERYONE*

**POETRY NOW 2003** - Any subject, any style, any time.

**WOMENSWORDS 2003** - Strictly women, have your say the female way!

**STRONGWORDS 2003** - Warning! Age restriction, must be between 16-24, opinionated and have strong views.
(Not for the faint-hearted)

All poems no longer than 30 lines.
Always welcome! No fee!
Cash Prizes to be won!

Mark your envelope (eg *Poetry Now*) *2003*
Send to:
Forward Press Ltd
Remus House, Coltsfoot Drive,
Peterborough, PE2 9JX

**OVER £10,000 POETRY PRIZES TO BE WON!**

Judging will take place in October 2003